# A
# YACHTSMAN'S
# TALE

By

Harry the 'B' Horne

For those who have not served onboard Britannia or in the Royal Navy, a list of essential abbreviations and general 'Jack Speak' can be found at the back of the book

Photographs by Snaps, Snaps and Snaps

PRINTED BY ORBITAL PRINT, DIGITAL DIVISION
STAPLEHURST ROAD, SITTINGBOURNE, KENT, ME10 2NH
LITHO DIVISION, ORBITAL PARK
ASHFORD, KENT, TN24 OGA

ISBN    978 1 62407 420 2

This book is dedicated to all yachtsmen who I had the pleasure of serving with, but most of all, for those that have since passed over the bar – God bless you all

## About Harry the B

I was born in the village of St Peters near Broadstairs on the Isle of Thanet in The Garden of England, Kent. I received the minimum education required and left school one week before my fifteenth birthday in 1969. I took a succession of jobs from apprentice ladies hairdresser (a skill that would stand me in good stead on Britannia) to a trainee wages clerk, with a few other mundane jobs in between.

My father a dustman/ labourer, and my mother a part time schools kitchen worker and night time laundry worker, a step brother in a special needs school, an elder sister and brother, and my twin. Both parents on miserable wages and with a lot of mouths to feed, but as I remember it, it was a wonderful childhood.

When my sister started courting a sailor, both my twin and I thought it could be the life for us. We would join the Navy together, but be accepted into service three months apart. I would go onto serve in Frigates- Ice Patrol Ship Endurance – be land based in the Falklands and recalled for active service in Kosovo with the Army, but most of all I would serve a total of twelve and a half years onboard Her Majesty's Yacht Britannia.

# ROYAL YACHT VOLUNTEER REQUIRED

When the signal was received in May 1985 onboard HMS Hermione a frigate based in Plymouth, asking for volunteers of the Stores Accounting Branch of Leading Hand Rate, my Chief Petty Officer Tom Scadden thought I should apply. I was less than happy on Hermione and without a second thought put in my request form. This was accepted and I set about finding out, as much as possible, about the most prestigious ship in the world.

I was put in the direction of a fellow Leading Stores Accountant Ron Camp as he had served onboard, leaving only when he had an unfortunate accident involving a ladder stanchion and his wedding tackle; he was a mine of information and humorous stories, and the best of which involved the Royal Train. It appears that Ron had caught the extra duty of being Royal Train door opener at South Railway Jetty in Portsmouth Dockyard. Her Majesty would alight the train at a spot on the jetty marked with a brass plate, and board Britannia for the annual Western Isles cruise. Ron stood on the spot and the train duly arrived, he sprang to attention opened the train door and saluted smartly awaiting for Her Majesty to disembark. Her remark to Ron was about her concern over small baggage left on the train, where upon he assured her that he would make sure everything followed. Princess Margaret alighted next, and according to Ron was slightly unsteady on her feet, and as she stepped out of the train lost her footing and grabbed Ron around the neck. Ron still having one arm at the salute and the other full of Royal train door held on for dear life, should the pair of them go over. 'I'm rather worried about the small baggage' the Princess said according to Ron. Very quietly Ron without thinking replied – I've just sorted that out with your sister Ma'am'. Luckily for Ron he wasn't overheard and he got away with it.

Time passed slowly awaiting the Yacht's decision, and eventually the signal came giving the order to attend an interview onboard Britannia at Royal Yacht moorings Whale Island Portsmouth. Having my suit cleaned and putting all ribbing aside from my mess mates, I prepared for the forthcoming grilling.

The 'Walk Ashore' as it was known – a row of pontoons leading out to Britannia - was a hive of activity with stores and sailors all in either blue serge bell bottom trousers and gym shoes, or overalls generally mucking in together trying to shift a mountain of gear by forming a human chain, handing boxes of all sizes one to the other. 'Take something with you shouted' a sailor. That's the way it worked on Britannia, so in No1 uniform, arm full of stores I made my way up the gangway.

I was met by Chief Stores Accountant Jake Wade, who conducted my first interview, things seemed positive.  Jake passed me then to the Deputy Supply Officer, where things could have gone better and finally to the Supply Officer/Admiral's Secretary. The interview went well until he asked his final question 'Why of all the volunteers should I pick you'? Because says I – 'I have a good service record', then without really thinking I said 'I am an all round good egg and snappy dresser'. That's it – I thought I'd blown it, but he laughed and informed me that the very first signature on my service certificates was his.  We had met in 1972 at HMS Raleigh, me as a new entry, him as my Divisional Officer.

Returning to Hermione the lads had put a 'By Royal Appointment' sign over my bunk. The signal confirming that I was to join came shortly after, so I set about finding Ron Camp, who reckoned he could get me a social visit onboard one lunchtime.  True to his word the following week, I was going up the gangway again.

First stop onboard was the clothing store where I was measured for my uniforms by the guy I was to take over from; these he assured me would be waiting for me when I joined. Next stop the Unwinding Room, a unique facility of a bar run by the Yachtsmen for the Yachtsmen themselves. I was introduced to a couple of people I would be working with Dinger and Andy, and a pint was swiftly put in my hands.

Ron Camp must have been a very popular person when serving onboard, before long he was the centre of attention once again telling his story of 'Dress Ship'. This was the practise of raising flags from stem to stern and between all three masts, something I would get to know very well over the coming years. The flags from foc'sle to foremast were raised from the foc'sle, the flags between fore and main were pulled out of the funnel, and from aft to mainmast were raised from the Royal deck. Leaving only the ones from quarterdeck to after mast, which were raised off the quarterdeck. It appears that this time Ron who was on the Royal deck ready to attach the shackle at its required length, was prevented from doing so by the fact that all the strain in the cable had been taken up on the quarterdeck, this left Ron and his team with all the weight of the cable and wet flags on his pull line. Thinking no more about it, Ron shouts down 'Are you '@*!!'S' going to give me some slack or what'. Aft of the Royal deck is the very private area of Britannia known as the verandah deck, unfortunately for Ron Her Majesty just happened to be on deck at that moment. Looking above and all around her for the culprit, Ron had just enough time to duck away. It was probably just as well that Ron was due to have his nether regions collision with the ladder stanchion, his luck could not have held out for much longer, but also I felt Ron never let the truth get in the way of a good story.

# FALL FRONT TROUSERS AND GYMSHOES

I joined the Royal Yacht just as she returned from her annual cruise of the Western Isle of Scotland. She was busy preparing for a West Indies Royal Duty that was to last for three weeks. With most Yachtsmen soon to proceed on summer leave, the task of storing fell to the few that had had already had advance leave – oh and me!

Trying to take everything in that first morning was a bit of a headache – not only was I trying to find my way around in what seemed a rabbit warren, without the aid of location markings; the hardest part was going to be remembering everyone's name. Unlike any other ship in the fleet, ranks in the lower deck were not used as a form of address, no name tallies or branch badges were worn; I was introduced to at least five guys named Dave, three Rogers, two Swampies, a white chap affectionately called Nigs, and a Wiggy!

I was happy for two reasons during the first couple of weeks, glad to be off Hermione and proud to be on Britannia. I had been nicknamed 'Harry the Bastard' since my first day onboard thanks to the TV programme 'The Young One's'. This was shortened to Harry the B and would stick with me for the next twelve years. I would get used to the nickname but the trousers which had no zip, just buttons across the top and the wearing of old fashioned 'plimsolls'' known as Jimmys and worn without socks, would take a little longer. Having been blessed with sweaty feet my footwear would have to be scrubbed daily, not just to keep them white, but to keep the fellows I lived with from mutinying when I took them off. The purpose of the Jimmys was to avoid black marks from footwear on otherwise unmarked teak decks, and also to reduce the noise of foot traffic when passing over the Royal Apartments.

# FOUR O'CLOCK CLUB

With Britannia being a permanently Portsmouth based ship, most of the Yacht's company lived ashore, married or not. The evenings were quiet with only victualled members, me being one of them and the 'Duty Watch/Fire and Emergency Party' left onboard. Before leaving to go home for the evening some Yachties would avail themselves of a pint of draught beer in the Unwinding Room, the pubs at this time in Portsmouth didn't open until five. If Norrie the Cox'n or any other Senior Yachtsmen looked in and found someone sat there with a pint with a head on it before bar opening times 'Frothy Beer' would be the shout, and you would have to explain how you got a head on your beer if you hadn't just poured it. When five o'clock came the bar would open for an hour and a half, thus allowing the duty barman to get a shower and supper before opening again from 1930 – 2130. Somehow getting a beer during legal opening times never held the excitement of having to use a spare key and Limbo under the bar with exactly the right money, so as not to put the till out. The amount of times that a Yachtsmen due to go home on the five o'clock Gosport Ferry was still inboard at 1930 never failed to amaze me. Not only must they have had understanding wives, but been addicted to reheated dinners.

## LEARNING THE ROPES

My first couple of weeks went well and like most people in a new job I was out to impress, and it wasn't just Jake the Chief, it was all the Yacht's company. With no Tannoy system and main broadcast alarm systems being tested every morning things were a lot quieter, and with the average age of people on board being the same as mine, I felt I was no longer the old man of the mess, as I had been on Hermione.

The almost celebrity status that people treated you with when they found out you were on the Royal Yacht, was at first almost embarrassing. For some reason they all expected you to have met the Royal Family and at the very least, taken tea with them. Not only had I not met them, I hadn't even seen them, and this wouldn't change until we commenced Royal Duty. This I learned would be the Yacht's equivalent of Action Stations on a warship. We had no guns to fire, for that wasn't the business Britannia was in. Main armament consisted of flags flying, band playing and ice chinking in the guest's glasses. Everyone had more than one job onboard during these evolutions, mainly on a volunteer basis. Compulsory roles would include 'Man Ship' where all available Yachtsmen would line the Yacht's side upon the first arrival and final departure of the Royal party. All commands were given in the form of Morse code for Man ship and would have to be learnt and the actual manning practised.

| Long Dash | - March on |
| Long Dash | - Turn outboard |
| Long dash two dots | - Stand at ease |
| Long dash one dot | - Attention |
| Long dash two dots | - Dismiss |

How simple could it be? Laugh I nearly wet myself!

The march down the Yacht's side was so slow that everyone would lose step and start shuffling and weaving like a Chinese dragon. This would not be found amusing by the Commander who would be observing the proceedings from the jetty. As these rehearsals would happen before every Royal Duty even a novice like me would soon get the hang of it. Being of small stature I would always be somewhere near the front of the dragon, and be within earshot of the very faint buzzer. Those of a taller disposition would not have the longest slow march to perform, but they were always further away from the buzzer. They would often turn and march off when the order was Stand at ease. At these times the Commander would lose his joke book, which only made it seem even funnier, and often as not we would find ourselves repeating the rehearsal time and time again. My other compulsory role was Dress Ship, which was not practised.

As the Yacht was Handraulic rather than Hydraulic it took lots of Hands to get the flags up without any hitches. My station would be Flag Deck, starboard side, pulling the flags out of the funnel with Jake Wade being in charge. This I was assured was an easy task if the guy in the funnel released the lines just before we started pulling, if not we would be trying to pull the funnel up as well as the flags. I would find out soon enough, but somehow I couldn't get Ron Camps reminiscence out of my mind.

The final introduction of any new Yachtsman before sailing was to look around the Royal apartments for fire fighting purposes, and as all equipment was secreted behind panels in the bulkheads, it was a mystery tour. My first impressions were how plain and tasteful the décor was, with plain white walls and simple furnishings. If anything impressed it was the artefacts that adorned the tables and hung on the bulkheads. All of these items had been gifted or donated to Her Majesty from every corner of the globe. A wooden shark from Pitcairn Island signed by all the descendants of the mutineers of HMS Bounty, a button from Lord Nelson's jacket, golden camels with rubies as dates hanging from palm trees. I would have to learn all their origins if I was ever going to give family or friends a tour. Lots of the crew made up stories about the artefacts, a sword from Sweden was often passed off as 'Excalibur' for a laugh.

# WEST INDIES 1985

Finally we were on our way; I only hoped that after the next couple of months I would be able to say to those that asked 'Yes – I've met the Royals'.  This nearly never came about at all, for as soon as we reached Bermuda I thought my Royal Yacht career was at an end. The day started normally enough, but the S & S were to finish early and have a bar b q on the local defence force beach, with a good time guaranteed beer, burgers and a bus to take us – what could go wrong?  I was on my best behaviour and the day went well, it was to be the short coach journey back to the Yacht that was to be my downfall.  The Caterer's assistant's name was Peter but no one ever called him by this; his nick name was Nigger or Nigs.  My offence was to actually call him by his nickname during a conversation on the bus that was being driven by a local defence force rating.  It was the following day that I found my Divisional Officer – Warrant Officer Rob White outside the clothing store wanting more than a quiet word. I had no defence – I had called Peter - Nigs, it didn't matter if I was in ear shot of the driver or not.   Fearing the worst I just waited to be thrown off, whilst keeping my head down, staying out of the bar and most of all – out of Rob's way.  It was Dinger who noticed that I had withdrawn and was no longer taking part having previously been the life and soul of the party; his advice was to shake this thing off and get over it, 'Stick with me and you won't go wrong' he said, 'for you always dip in with Dinger'. Her Majesty embarked in Nassau for the Heads of Governments meeting, and the days just got busier and busier.

## ROYAL ENCOUNTER

Probably the worst of all the extra jobs that the Stores department had, was taking charge of the umbrella party.  Every time a member of the Royal Family embarked or disembarked, waiting on the jetty or hidden away in what we knew as the forward cross passage, waited the umbrella party on stand by. There wouldn't be a cloud in the sky some days, but getting a decision out of the Officer of the day, or the duty Commander to stand the lads down very rarely came, and at certain times we became known as the parasol party. The reluctance to dispense with the umbrella party was understandable; at times it could start and stop raining without any warning. As I stood on the jetty soaking wet, umbrella under my arm waiting for the Royals to arrive, the car turned the corner the rain stopped and the sun came out. This left me in a bit of a dilemma; the decision to do nothing was an easy one to come to. With both the Queen and the Duke at arm's length I just stood there and looked straight ahead, they must have thought someone had chucked a bucket of water over me, as even the car door openers were held back until the rain had subsided.

## DIPPING IN WITH DINGER

I made sure that if I went ashore again it was with Dinger, and it wasn't long before we were the best of friends. His infectious sense of humour and the ability to raise either eyebrow independently never failed to amuse, so when he said we're off to a party being hosted by the head of the Bank of Nova Scotia, having met them earlier in the day. I was not surprised. Also attending was a lady who was connected to the Avon Rubber Company by birth or marriage. During the war she delivered Spitfires from the manufacturers to their home bases. She told the most wonderful story of how when delivering one such aircraft she came across a couple of Fockers, by which she meant Fockerwolfe German fighter planes. Before she could continue Dinger piped up and said 'Bloody Hell I didn't know we could swear'. The ice was immediately broken and an evening

that had been a little stuffy turned into a corker.  Being offered the
pool to have a dip, quick as a flash, we were down to our underwear
and formation swimming whilst humming "New York – New York"
underwater. By the sound of their laughter they had as good an
evening as we did. With the Royal Duty sometimes taking in two
islands a day, runs ashore were few and far between, but if an
opportunity arose I took it.

In St Vincent taking in the sun on a hotel beach, we were approached
by a London publican, who being on an all inclusive holiday was
being very generous with the beer.  Watching how much you
consumed on Royal Duty was a must, the penalty for returning to
Britannia intoxicated were severe, paying for your own flight home
was a high price for a few free beers. We were getting on well with
our publican friend when out of the bushes came a rather drunk
Yachtsman by the name of Yorkie Hallet shouting 'I've lost my
bloody Grippo'. With just a glance at each other we knew it was time
to leave.  Yorkie was not destined to serve very long on Britannia,
and I believe that even he knew it.

The temptation to run amok on the islands would have been greater,
had we spent more time alongside. I had in the seventies served on
HMS Eskimo a Tribal Class Frigate acting as West Indies Guard
ship, which visited every island, over a deployment of ten months, so
at least I knew what was ashore.  Some of the Royal Stewards who
worked flat out, never got down the gangway at all, and as one lad
put it 'I came, I saw, but unfortunately only out of the scuttle'.
It was a great relief when Royal Duty came to an end, just to get my
kit sorted out. The After Mess looked like a bomb had gone off with
uniforms hanging everywhere.  It was not unusual to get through
three different rigs in one day, shorts, blues and full white No 6
tropicals.  With over forty people in the Mess and no more room than

a warship to stow your gear, it just seemed to spread. The laundry would be flat out for some time yet.

## BEER FROM A WATER FOUNTAIN

Something new to me was all the rounds of 'thank you' drinks that were handed out by all the departments, the quarterdeck would be the venue for the larger groups such as sports teams and supporters. The Water Cooler situated in the main passage way between the Chief's and Petty Officer's messes was the venue for smaller parties. There was always something to celebrate, birthdays, anniversaries and most of all successful Royal Duties, getting in on the invite was the tricky bit. Working in the Stores I soon became known and it wasn't long before I was in all the cliques. I'm sure this didn't go unnoticed by Rob White, who always seemed to pass when I was stood there.

## CHRISTMAS 1985

I always suspected that as I was the last man in, I would be elected to keep the forthcoming Christmas Duties, an inconvenience if nothing else. As all major storing would be completed before main leave commenced, all that would be required of me would be a set of rounds of the storerooms, and the provision of food to the galleys on a daily basis. Andy the Caterer and Dinger would come to my rescue, providing cover for Christmas and Boxing Day, and at the weekends I would make the 140 mile journey each way and still be home for lunch. I could not have foreseen I would be doing this with my leg strapped up, having missed the last couple of rungs of a ladder outside the Unwinding Room. Small amounts of stores arrived on a daily basis and would have to be transported up the Walk Ashore. Luckily a Killick sailor called Bluey took care of this, ferrying all the gear by his inflatable boat, normally used as a paint punt. With a more than helpful Duty watch, the gear very soon found its way inboard. The heaviest and most dreaded of all stores arriving was the Naafi stores. 500 barrels of beer and lager in five gallon kegs all had to be manhandled up the gangway, down through the bowels of the Yacht, to the plumber's shop, where one by one they were lowered into the forepeak. A full load would take two full days to strike down below, and you could see the relief on everyone's face when the last barrel disappeared down through the hatch. In comparison a thousand crates of canned beer and lager could be struck into the unused garage in just a few hours. The garage had at one times held a Rolls Royce of unique dimensions, when the bumpers were taken off this could be fitted in sideways, using special rails set into the boat deck. This I believe was such a performance it certainly never came onboard in my time. If luck was on our side the odd crate might hit the deck, and if the Naafi Manager was in a good mood, he might see fit to share the contents with the stores party. Any suggestion we would drop one on purpose would of course be true, and the hotter the day the more frequently it would happen.

## ANTIPODEAN DEPLOYMENT 1986

Sailing New Year's Eve took the smile away from lots of faces, partly because it was New Year's Eve, but also because it was blowing a Force Ten in the channel, and the long term forecast for the Bay of Biscay didn't look any better. The Unwinding Room on any day of sailing was normally full; tonight it would be a different story with the motion in the bows of Britannia being quite violent. Tables were turning over and the only safe place to sit was on the deck, unless of course you were involved in 'Bunny Hopping'. This involved timing you jump to perfection, you had to go up as the Yacht's bows came down, and you could stay airborne almost glued to the deck head for a good couple of seconds. Only thing required is a clear landing site, and a safe place to stow your beer. Ron the Butcher decided to join us, but refused to sit on the deck. Ron was the oldest man in the lower deck and certainly the oldest serving Royal Marine. Ron had only been seated a short while when Britannia lurched catapulting Ron from the starboard side to find himself bouncing off the trophy cabinets on the port side, and of course needing stitches. He was lucky to have missed the glass trophy cabinet doors; otherwise he would have needed more serious medical attention.

The weather stayed rough well into the Mediterranean, and much needed hard work would have to be done on the rusty patches that always appeared after a prolonged spell of bad weather. It's amazing how many people volunteered for jobs on the upper deck when the sun is shining, but only after the Buffer has put it out of bounds. Off watch chefs, stokers, bandies and even the odd day worker would be out with a can of Brasso and a polishing cloth, stripped to the waist absorbing the sunshine. The Foc'sle during the sunshine hours was known as the wooden beach, an approved sun bathing area for Yachtsmen who varied in shade from anaemic to red. During the hours of darkness it would be the venue for various 'bucket parties'. With the temperature below decks getting hotter, the practise of filling a bucket with Ice and beer, kicking off your flip flops and just chilling out occupied most people's evenings. The lucky ones would come back and find their footwear intact, the unlucky one's would find a bite sized chunk missing, it was 'Ugly Balster the Royal Steward's' trademark.

## OPERATION BALZAC

Balls ache might have been a more appropriate name, stuck as we were at the mouth of the Red Sea, only able to look at the ocean that stretched ahead of us and the cooling breezes that it would bring. We seemed to have been hanging around with only the odd buzz filtering through the lower deck as to what was going on. Something was seriously amiss ashore; we could see that from all the various smoke trails that lined the shore. The first of so many Red Hots were quickly distributed to messes and notice boards by Tom the Coxn's runner. These chits of paper were our only source of information from Command, and soon made redundant by regular updates by the rarely used Yacht's internal speaker system. Civil uprising ashore in Aden had left, not just British, but many Nationalities stranded and wanting to get out of what was now a war zone.

The Royal Stewards had been busy turning the Royal Apartments from a place of grace and splendour into a dormitory with all the spare bedding that was held onboard. Mattresses were proving to be the only problem, and at one time the crew thought that we were going to have to give up our own. This would not have proved a popular move as the cleanliness of some of the refugees that we would be picking up was more than just suspect. With everything of value stowed away in the Yacht's hold, we were ready to start ferrying refugees as and when they arrived at the beaches. Getting to them was proving to be the hard part and much liaison was going on between the Embassy staff ashore and our own Command. I did not envy Rear Admiral Garnier one bit, being in charge of Britannia must have been at times like driving a very valuable vintage car into a banger race. If we were approaching a beach he made sure there was little or no chance of us taking a hit, freak shot or otherwise. It was decided to land Lieutenant Easson and a radio operator, to act as beach marshal, although armed with a 9mm pistol his main armament turned out to be a box of Mars Bars. These he handed out to all the Arabs and by all accounts they proved to be very popular, and I believe more were sent ashore at regular intervals. We started ferrying refugees off the beaches using our own boats. The only one to stay on its davits was the Royal Barge, not even FORY wanted this one damaged.  During the whole operation I was stationed in the Stores Office with just the broadcast and the odd phone call to keep me informed.  I was a mushroom in every sense of the word, being kept in the dark with dead lights down over scuttles, I couldn't even see what was going on outside.  I had given away every article of useful clothing that could be used from the clothing store, so felt there was now little more use that could be made of me.  Jake did phone down and ask me up to the Sun Lounge which was being used to process all refugees.  If one nationality had to be singled out for special praise, it would be the Chinese, perfectly behaved and waiting in line to be registered.

With boats going in to safe beaches it wasn't long before we were full and on our way to Djibouti where we could drop off our passengers.  The relief on their faces said it all, and disbelief from amongst westerners that they were actually aboard Britannia.  Stories were not long coming from refugees about lost and left behind baggage; one from a chap who said he had buried in the sand a suitcase containing half a million dollars, perhaps it was covered by insurance, but I wonder if he ever returned on holiday taking just a spade. (Certainly the incentive you need to holiday in what is now the Yemen).  We would make the round trip from Aden to Djibouti usually during the night, returning time and time again until the final count of refugees exceeded one thousand from over fifty nationalities.  The whole episode which lasted nine days passed without Britannia getting a scratch, although it had taken its toll on both the boats and the lads.  One sailor 'Barty' who was Cox'n of a whaler known as a jolly boat thought he had been shot, only to find his self inflating lifejacket had got wet activating the air bottle which gave a loud crack before inflating the jacket tightly across his chest.  He was ribbed unmercifully for a few days by us all giving him something to moan about – Barty moaned a lot anyway.

If anyone dipped in at all over this period it could have only been Dinger. He formed part of the First Aid party down in the Royal apartments, and although only basic first aid was needed, for the more distressed refugees the lads were always on hand. We had on one trip picked up a rather good looking French lady complete with poodle, who insisted on having a shower. That didn't prove to be a problem as showers were something we had plenty of, and she soon availed herself of one of them. Emerging from her ablutions only to find no towel to dry herself, she decided to venture out and ask anyone she could find. Luckily for Dinger he was on hand, I say lucky for the lady was absolutely naked, and we had been at sea for the best part of a month. If I have one memory of Djibouti it is that each time we returned, most of the nationalities had been sorted out by their own embassies, but a few faces were still there after days. Thank God to be British.

With this delay to our programme the general feeling was that we may now turn around and head home, well at least we hoped we would. We had made the news on every channel and on every night, even the papers were being kind to us, not something they had been in the past. If we turned around it would have been the first time in Britannia's history that she had missed a Royal Duty, and that wasn't about to happen. By cutting short our time alongside, for fuelling and a run ashore to just a day in Singapore, Darwin and Cairns, it was estimated we would reach New Zealand on time and be ready. There were those amongst the crew that thought our sailing date of New Years Eve and our involvement in the Aden evacuations were more than a coincidence, and no reasoning would change their minds. The clothing store had been full of general service No 8 uniforms (blue denim shirts and trousers) but this was for Yacht issue to Yachtsmen going on professional courses the following year. In Singapore it was decided to fumigate the Royal Apartments just to be on the safe side, this didn't delay us and as soon as the furniture, fixings and fittings were back in place, you would never have guessed what the Yacht had just been through.

## BOB THE BANDIE'S BIRTHDAY

The Yacht arrived in Auckland the day the Queen and the Duke landed, we had made it but there was lots of work to do before we could say we were up to scratch for Royal Duty.  Her Majesty embarked and immediately after Man Ship the Lower Deck was cleared to assist the sailors in rigging awnings over the verandah deck, she looked on in amusement as sailors wet and bedraggled hung on for dear life as canvasses flapped and threatened to take off. Two umbrellas turned inside out, and Nigs managed to stab the Duke in the back of the neck with his as the wind took it. The Duke was not amused.  With the Royals installed, and work out of the way, a group of us had decided to have a run ashore to celebrate Bob Simmons' birthday. Bob was probably the most popular bandsman, always in the Unwinding room and always on the piano on Sunday lunchtimes.  When Bob was playing Billy Joel's Root Beer rag he could bring the house down.  Auckland had shut in honour of the Queen's visit but we found a little club open called 'Steps' which had a live band.  During the interval Bob asked if he could play and as we were all in uniform, this was granted.  Bob played Billy Joel's Piano Man and we sang the lyrics, and it wasn't long before girls were standing all around Bob in groups three deep. He could have had his pick, but if Bob was good looking – he was also smooth. Excuse me girls he said 'my birthday round at the bar for the boys', took a drag on his cigarette, tucked his beret in his epaulette and made his way back to the bar.  Bob, like us, had a lady at home and never played the field, he must have upset a great many girls over the years.

# STREWTH

The term Strewth was an Australian one, made up of a girl's name mixed with a bit of emotion at first meeting her. Although 'Ruth' was a nice enough girl, her rotund frame and plain looks made her the original wall flower. I had met her ashore on our first night in Melbourne at the Police social club. Free beer and burgers meant it was oversubscribed and Norrie would have to make a draw out of a hat to see who went. Greeted by our hosts of Police and civilian workers, the party went into overdrive immediately. The term 'Pommie Bastard' was used to destruction with our only retort being; 'well at least my ancestors weren't criminals'. All very light-hearted banter, which I think the Aussies won. I was introduced to Ruth halfway through the evening whilst telling probably the same joke I had told ten minutes earlier, (I do this after a pint or two). Big girls do like a laugh and it seemed with Ruth, the ruder the better. The evening flew passed and we were put back on our coach, each being given a can of beer to provide sustenance for the long 30 minute journey back. Being on Royal Duty meant we could not return the hospitality, which probably saved us a fortune, as these Aussies could have done us severe financial damage at the bar. It was with much surprise the following day when I was called to the gangway, to meet a visitor at the main gate – **Strewth**! I was being invited to see the sights, call me a coward but I declined with much squirming and lie telling, but had to conceded to meeting her in a local bar that evening. Taking a couple of lads with me seemed prudent and at the end of the evening, I felt my duty had been done. Ruth had other ideas and turned up daily, I was being stalked by a rather large Sheila with a good sense of humour, so the Gangway staff and everybody else I knew were put on full 'Strewth alert', and my whereabouts were not to be revealed at any cost. I would be glad to leave Melbourne and Ruth well behind me.

# SEA DAYS AND RECEPTIONS

This was a new one on me, but had been going since the early 1980's. The term Sea Day's was used to describe Britannia doing her bit for Britain by promoting trade. The idea it seems to take British business representatives and their counterparts from whatever country we were visiting out to sea, proved to be a real popular one, multi million pound deals were signed on Britannia, and if we had any of the Royal Family onboard could be oversubscribed. Those that couldn't get onboard for the Sea Day would attend an evening reception, nibbles and plenty to drink, with The Royal Marine Band performing 'Beat The Retreat' on the jetty to finish off. These days could be busier than Royal Duty and volunteers were always required, some to help out in the pantries washing up, and some in the Royal Apartments serving the reception guests. I had worked as a silver service waiter on Townsend ferries in the late seventies, but kept this to myself, preferring to wash up. This most mundane of tasks was essential as Britannia had no automatic dishwashers, so all the valuable glass and porcelain had to be done by hand to avoid breakages. The perks of this most coveted of jobs paid what was known as 'Green Cloth Money' a payment so small from the Palace funds it didn't even come into the equation. Most, if not all, of the volunteers were there for a beer and a laugh, and of course the thank you drinks on the quarterdeck at the end of the deployment. The temperatures in the wash up being well into the nineties, you would sweat any beers off with no problem at all. With Royal Duty behind us, now would come the long trek home; we would be at sea with only the odd day or two alongside for fuel and a run ashore for the best part of six weeks. What started as a pastime between Dinger, Smurf and me in the clothing store was now seriously getting out of hand. Since leaving Aden the three of us had taken to having a guitar session for a couple of hours every evening. With Smurf already being an accomplished player, and Dinger certainly well on the way, I became their student.

## THE TONE DEAF'S

There was talk of a forthcoming concert on the quarterdeck, with support from the Royal Marine band that had been given the go ahead to last all evening. We were given top billing and not to hit the stage until about 2100, presumably to allow the audience to have a tin or two and appreciate our efforts more. We still had a couple of weeks to prepare our act and decide upon its content. With only Dinger having a singing voice, we decided to recruit a backing group, the only volunteers for the job being, Jerry, Bob, Spider and Jim, they were to be called 'The Adrifters' as we didn't require them until after our opening song. A big entrance was sorted out; the Tone Deafs would come up out of the quarterdeck hatch, whilst the Adrifters would join us by means of the verandah deck. The day was soon upon us and preparations for lighting and bar were well under way. Norrie had agreed ten crates could be sold on the quarterdeck using a 50 gallon potato bin full of ice to keep it chilled. This would save Yachtsmen running up and down to the Unwinding Room every time they needed a refill. Two stokers, Snowy and Keo, started the ball rolling with a bit of country music, and the band played until our time arrived. To chants of 'Tone Deafs, Tone Deafs' we entered to tremendous applause, we started our first song from Billy Joel. If we didn't have their full attention when we started, we certainly got it when we sang the line 'Turn out the lights' and Barry and Alf the electricians did, plunging the quarterdeck into darkness. Great effect, but now we could no longer see the words and the band couldn't see the music. Recovering quickly we received tremendous applause from the crowd, who even at this time had exhausted the beer, which Nigs was quickly replenishing from the garage. Introducing the

Adrifters who weren't there as planned got a laugh, but their costumes and blacked out faces brought the house down. Spider with his first line 'Don't sit on the grass man – Smoke it' raised an eyebrow or two and from there it was all downhill. Next number 'True' by Spandau Ballet, with their voices at full stretch singing 'Aah-Aah-Aah-Aah' you really couldn't hear above the laughter, not what Dinger had planned at all, he was taking all of this very seriously, as it was his solo. When the laughter subsided things started to improve but only because of the aid of our professional bandsmen, Sid, Dick, Hammy, Bogie and Bob the man on the organ that provided every sound effect from bells to whistles. Good gig guys.

## CROSSING THE LINE

I guess we should have had the 'Crossing the Line 'ceremony on the way south, but it really didn't matter. All those that had not crossed the Equator before would be in for a dunking. On any other ship it was the quickest of affairs and hardly any ceremony at all. Britannia would put on a show that took a whole afternoon; I'd wished that I hadn't crossed the line a few times before, so that I could be part of it, if only for the certificate. Norrie would be Neptune or his Missis, a role befitting his stature, and Rob would always be Clerk of the Court as he owned the wig and barristers outfit; role of the barbers went to the shipwrights, and the Doc's to the Sick Bay team. The Bears (the guys that you were thrown to, were hopefully the biggest guys onboard, the regulars being Barry, Alf, Andy T, Frenchie, Ugly and the odd Marine). On any other ship it was to read the charge, then into the canvas bath for a quick dunking– and that's the lot, bring on the next victim, with the Yacht you could expect a double dunking at least as two canvas baths were always set up, and if the crowd bayed for more – you'd go round twice. I didn't see anybody drown but it was a close run thing.

# ANNOUNCEMENTS AND DECISIONS

With the Tone Deafs first and last concert out of the way, I had packed away the guitar and picked up my books to study for the next higher rate of Petty Officer. All was going well and I felt sure I would be ready to take my exams on our next deployment. Only two things could possibly upset my plans and with all the buzzes going around it looked like it was going to happen. The marriage of the Duke of York had been announced, and as with all other Royal marriages the Royal Yacht was likely to be required for the honeymoon. This was going to make what was an already very busy year even busier. I had planned a holiday with my partner Kay, but with a change of programme, it meant that we would not be off at the same time. Relationships would be strained to the limit. Dinger flew off to take advance leave, and would be waiting on the jetty upon our arrival back in Pompey. Proceeding on leave as soon as we docked, I laid the master plan at Kay's feet. Although I was more than happy on Britannia, there was only one way I could see more of her, and that was to apply for submarine service. You could have heard a pin drop. Kay had never interfered with my naval career, on the contrary she was the reason I had rejoined and has given me much support and advice over the years. I thought about my decision in two ways financial and geographical, money was after all the only reason I was at sea. Submarine pay even at this time was a couple of hundred pounds a month more, and the submarines I was going to volunteer for ran out of Portsmouth. The decision to award the forthcoming ten month refit to Plymouth Dockyard also went completely against the grain, more separation and lots of travelling to get home for weekends. Seventy percent of the Yacht's company lived and had family in the Portsmouth area, they were livid, and many an old Yachtsman handed in a request to return to general service. My mind was made up; even though Rob White had warned me it would take longer to get me off Britannia than it took to get me on. So not only would I end up doing the Honeymoon and the next Far East deployment, I could expect to serve some time in Plymouth. At the Commander's table Rob had few words to say, except when asked if I was recommended for submarine service his answer being ' highly Sir – he's exactly the size their looking for'.

## AZORES HONEYMOON

Eight weeks in Portsmouth passed in a flash and Britannia was once more heading out to sea. We would be the target for every camera and reporter who was hoping for a quick scoop. First stop Victoria Terceira where we anchored and awaited the Duke and Duchess of York. Britannia must have looked splendid to the new Duchess dressed overall and the crew lining the decks at Man Ship stations. The game of cat and mouse with the press started for real, they had acquired every boat that was available for hire. We upped anchor and sped off hiding as best we could amongst the islands, but being 125 metres long this was not easy. Darkness was to be our best ally over the next week ensuring that the Duke and Duchess had privacy. Water sports figured highly on the agenda every day with both Royals water skiing and sun bathing on deck. Our wooden beach was open to all 'two foot Yachtsmen'. Providing your head never came above the gunwales, whilst the Royals were in sight, you were welcome to use the deck. A walk round by the Royals of Britannia, to meet the crew, was the highlight of the trip for me, and for the first time I could say that not only had I met a Royal, I'd had a chat as well.

## COWES

With an aquatic welcome to greet us, we entered Cowes and promptly dropped anchor. The flotilla of tiny boats bobbing around our bows like dolphins at play must have been the Commander's nightmare, how none of them got run over by Britannia's 5500 tons is amazing. Liberty boat routine meant even making a phone call could take a couple of hours, and with little else to do a couple of pints and fish and chips would be the order of the day. Cowes was assigned a Guard Ship normally a frigate, that would find the whole thing as mundane as us, if you were not of the yachting scene there was very little in the way of entertainment. You could always spot a Yachtsman ashore, shirt and tie worn at all times. We were again a target for the press, still trying to get the latest about the honeymoon. We would find sanctuary in the British Legion, which at this time became the Unwinding Room ashore.

If anything caught me by surprise it was being detailed as the Standby LSA to sit onboard the racing yacht 'Yeoman 21' overnight. After the Duke of Edinburgh had finished racing, the Yacht was moored empty in the Medina River and required a security sentry. Evidently this task had fallen to the Jack Dusties after 'Steve Gibson' from the stores branch a keen fisherman, had volunteered. So many tasks had fallen to different branches in this way. Being given some advice by Andy who had done the job every Cowes week for years, he said 'just ask them where the beer is -16 hours is a long watch'. I did just that and found copious amounts in the sail locker as directed. Armed with a miniature television, the screen the size of a matchbox, I was set for a long evening and an even longer night. The liberty boat ran from Britannia at regular intervals, and would always make a pass to ensure everything was okay. At other times they would just pass and create a wake, which would leave you bobbing up and down as you watched them wave their fish and chips at you. Not all the boat crews were as cold hearted, some would stop and pass something from the chip shop normally purchased and sent on by mess mates. Sleep was impossible with the rattling of the masts and the general dampness below decks; I hoped I would not get this duty more than once. I must have nodded off for I awoke to the sounds of scratching on the hull, not having been given anything, not even a stick to ward anyone off with, could be a problem. I needn't have worried as it was only the Yacht's divers doing their morning search on the hull for mines. Bloody marvellous, here they are checking for explosives that may have been planted overnight. How expendable it made one seem. Cowes was a drag if you lived onboard, but for those with homes ashore they would be on the D52 dockyard boat ferry on a daily basis, arriving onboard at 0800 and on the next boat back at 1230 on a daily basis, although some would love to deny it.

## WESTERN ISLES

This I was informed was the Queen's favourite time to be onboard, getting any official engagements out of the way during the passage up north and then, relaxing. The crew would amuse themselves if not involved with the Royal party, by fishing off of the foc'sle. Amazing how many Yachtsmen had a passion for the rod and line, hanging over the ships side with expectant looks. They pulled up fish by the score, so many in fact the Caterer was being plagued for space in the yacht's freezers. With so many fishing lines dangling outside the Unwinding Room scuttles; the pastime would be to see how many beer cans could be attached without disturbing the rod, giving a pull on the line only when we had finished, and then running to the foc'sle to find out who the owner was. A walk ashore was occasionally on offer, sometimes even a Bar B Q on a beach well away from the Royal party. The Duke was normally in charge of the Royal Bar B Q and all the kindling would be cut to his exact requirements by the Shipwrights. This should have lit quite easily had they not used fire retardant off cuts on one occasion, causing much frustration to the Duke and embarrassment to the Chippies.

The routine wouldn't change from day to day, with the Queen being briefed on the weather and our course plotted to pick up the best of it. Finding sunshine and dodging showers was sometimes a thankless task, leaving the Royals with the choice to walk ashore in the wet or remain onboard. I won the umbrella party duty on one occasion; standing on the lowered accommodation ladder when Her Majesty appeared in full waterproof gear, saying 'I don't require an umbrella' yet again I was soaked to the skin in full No 1 uniform. The Royals would disembark at Aberdeen and head off to Balmoral, whilst we would fuel and take on as much fish as could be got in the freezers, and get a well earned run ashore. A tradition between the Queens's flight and Britannia was to exchange half a dozen Yachtsmen who would fly south in the Queens Flight, and six RAF would sail down to Portsmouth with us. It was only a couple of days sailing south but to the Queen's Flight, everything was free. They exploited this to the full and partied all the way down, and if any fell asleep in the Unwinding Room they could expect to wake up missing an eyebrow, moustache and even their uniform, which went out the scuttle. They loved it, and many good friends were made in the Queen's Flight over the years, who we would only see at the annual RAF Benson verses Royal Yacht sports day.

## FAR FLUNG 1986

Four weeks in Portsmouth and we were off again, all this sea time was starting to take its toll. Still never mind we were on our way to China, and would be back for Christmas, so it wasn't all bad. The journey out as always meant cleaning and more cleaning until the Yacht shone inside and out; even compartments like the Rag store would be reported for Commanders rounds, and have to be up to scratch. No dust on the overhead fan trunkings or cable tracks (and this is a rag store!). Finally the Admiral would have his Rounds, and we could start to relax just a bit. Taking fuel in Gibraltar, Port Said and Colombo offered the much needed run ashore, but it was to be Singapore that would be the highlight of the trip east. Shopping trips down Orchard Road and Change Alley keeping us amused during the day, and Semberwang Village and the Terror Club taking our time in the evenings. Only four of the original bars are now open, the village just being a shadow of its former self. I'd made it through a monsoon one evening to the Cowboy Bar and was drying off, when Nigs came in soaked to the skin, and looking like he'd done three rounds with Henry Cooper. Head down running through the rain, he'd gone head first into a three foot deep monsoon ditch; 'well if nothing else' he said 'that's sobered me up'.

The Lady Boys that used to act as hostesses were now very thin on the ground, and those that did still hang around had to be women, they were far too ugly to be men. Our expert on all things Eastern was a guy who had joined us in Portsmouth before sailing named Tony Pinnock, nicknamed 'Two Sheds' as he had two places of work. He was a regular for a run ashore. Having served in Hong Kong Tony could ask for a beer in Mandarin and Cantonese, and being short of arms and deep in pocket, he could also say in both languages 'My friend will pay'. The traders on the Jetty were doing a brisk trade in porcelain elephants and concrete dragon pots; these seemed to be coming over the gangway in vast amounts. The dockyard had, prior to sailing, sealed and flooded a storeroom located below the Main Naval Store to combat the ever increasing weight of paint on the super structure. Looking at how low Britannia was now floating in the water due to all this new cargo, they shouldn't have bothered. I did get the feeling, seeing all this coming onboard, that I would soon be asked if I had room in my clothing store. Space was certainly at a premium, you couldn't walk into any compartment without finding someone's treasured 'Rabbits' all wrapped and named, but mostly in the way. I rearranged the clothing store and found room for a couple of herds of elephants and enough pots to line the Burma Road; it no longer looked like a store, more like Susie Wong's Bazaar.

## NOT ANOTHER TATTOO

This was my first time in Hong Kong. The China Fleet Club and a visit to 'Pinkies' used to be a sailor's run ashore, but I'd already got Tattoos and promised that enough was enough. I Followed Dinger in who had planned to have his 'Saturday Night's all Right for Fighting tattoo' over done with something more suitable. Having found Pinkies it was difficult to get in for the sea of Yachtsmen who were lined up inside waiting in turn to disfigure the strangest parts of their bodies. Moby from the sail makers shop was having a bird on his buttock pulling a worm out of his sphincter, others were having a stoker on one cheek stoking a fire, with an Angel on the other with a fire extinguisher, and flames erupting from the very sensitive bit in the middle – ouch! How I got talked into one I'm not quite sure but having in Cantonese tattooed on my shoulder 'My dear love Kay', I didn't realize how much distress it would cause her. With my medical for submarine service due to be done in HMS Tamar, Hong Kong's shore base, our very nice medical staff also arranged a blood test, the first of few that Kay would demand I take. Since I last had a tattoo in the early seventies, someone had invented Aids, and Kay was right to be wary of it.

I had taken my exams for Petty Officer on our way across the Indian Ocean. Results were in and I had passed, along with my blood test proving negative and having passed my submarine medical, triple celebrations were on the cards. Although the more I thought about submarines the less it appealed to me, but things had moved on so much now, and it was a roller coaster that wouldn't stop. Putting all this out of my mind, I concentrated on the next stop; China how anyone could not be excited.

## SHANGHAI

With a clear five day's alongside before Royal Duty there was some serious sightseeing to be done, and some even more serious shopping. It appeared the place for bargains was The Friendship Store where they would take credit cards, which for some people must by now be reaching their limit. Chinese rugs, camphor wood chests and cork carvings by the dozen, even bicycles were coming over the gangway and being stored up the funnel and in machinery spaces, we would sink I was sure of it. Tours by train into China's interior were on offer at bargain rates, with the only drawback being all tours started from the train station at 0500. With the only nightlife being in the Peace Hotel where they played the same Jazz music they had for the last forty years, you were forgiven for giving it a miss and staying onboard. The train station even at such an early hour was a heaving mass of bodies, crammed into carriages like sardines, certainly it looked like there would be no room for forty of Britain's little Ambassadors all dressed in full No 1 uniform. Much to our surprise a couple of First Class carriages were shunted around the station and attached to the rear of the train. For the entire journey we would be treated like VIP's. I'm not sure that when the drinks trolley came round it was a wise move to start on the beer, but I wasn't going to be the only one to be drinking tea with 'Tatlow the Matlot' who was Buffer at the time. Our destination was a town called Hanzoy, which turned out to be a fair distance away, our journey only being broken by a magnificent banquet at a Hotel. Once at our destination it was temples and silk factories, and the chance of some green tea. It was a relief to be back on the train where even the

Buffer had his lips around more than one can of beer, although not at the same time.

With a successful Sea Day Their Majesty's embarked and it was work as normal for us, but the Duke was keeping his head down after his 'Slitty Eyes' gaff. A comment he must have regretted as soon as it left his lips. With only a couple of days in Shanghai and bad weather, our departure was a very wet affair, the jetty that was meant to have seen hundreds of children singing and dancing was deserted. Our visit in Canton saw us berthed at the back of a container port and no shore leave granted. The Royals walking the Great Wall and seeing the Terracotta Army were kept very busy making all the crew envious. The send off from Canton was the most spectacular display; all the children must have been shipped down from Shanghai so as not to disappoint them and her Majesty; everything from dragons to dancing lions. The crew were allowed to watch from the boat deck, but as always no cameras, this rule was always strongly enforced ensuring no unofficial pictures of the Royals were ever taken onboard. Shiner Wrightson, 'Snaps' as the photographer is known, was going to be a busy lad for days to come. The journey over to Hong Kong was broken only by us taking refuge by Lamma Island, so Her Majesty who is not the best sailor would be more comfortable. We would make our way home stopping for fuel in Singapore and Colombo, before heading up to Matrah for our final Royal Duty with the Prince and Princess of Wales.

## SHEIKHS ALIVE

We arrived a full day before the Royals which gave both Stewards and Sailors time to prepare their parts of ship for the huge banquet that had been planned. With the Sailors it would be putting up the awnings over the verandah deck, and the never ending job of polishing the bright work. As standby LSA once again I was to draw the short straw, and was detailed off, this time to greet guests for the Banquet / Royal reception at the dockyard main gate, with the sole purpose of reminding them to take their invitations with them up the gangway, so they could be properly announced. Armed with a small two way radio, I set off for the main gate situated about a mile away, arriving at least an hour before any guests were due to arrive. A couple of sailors from our escort ship were already there, but unfortunately were giving me a complete blank, probably holding me personally responsible for the position they were finding themselves in. Listening to their tales of woe, of how busy their schedule was I should feel sorry for them, but for the fact we had been away from home twice as long as they had this year alone. I did feel for them though when they explained their command had made them paint their steaming boots white to match their white overalls. It wouldn't be the first time some skipper had over reacted to being Royal Guard ship, but this was certainly a new one on me. The first of the banquet guests arrived and cars were being driven slow enough, to be stopped and the invitation rule explained. As the time got later we noticed that the cars were going faster, and were a lot more reluctant to stop. The decision to stand in the road was made, but after flapping my hands about and nearly being run over, it was quickly dismissed as a bad idea. The Arab gate staff were springing to attention and saluting every time a Rolls Royce was sighted, this was not giving the drivers the signal we wanted. With a success rate of stopping one car in five, I didn't think we were doing too badly, unfortunately the voice on the radio didn't agree 'Try harder' it said, and I was back in the middle of the road. When the last of the guests sped past at about 60mph, we thought we could stand down and return onboard. The Guard ship lads did just that, leaving me alone to handle the reception guests. The whole episode repeated itself only with the added hazard of darkness and lack of back up. I was finally given the okay to return onboard at 2200 hours. I had been out there for over six hours with no water, and had long since run out of cigarettes. Norrie was at the top of the brow with an apology and a couple of beers, he had assumed I would be in need of refreshment. He was right, the last message of any importance that the two way radio sent, was via the Quarter Master to the duty barman, where I booked last orders, I now had half a dozen tins to see off before bed time – funny old game isn't it!

## CAKE MIX, RADIO RECEPTION AND RAFFLES

It has always been Yacht tradition during the last Royal Duty to mix the Christmas cake, aided of course by the last Royal's onboard that year. This year it would fall to The Prince and Princess of Wales, with the chefs being the lucky ones to really get involved in a bit of banter. Although the Royals administered one bottle, of brandy another was always added later to give the cake a bit of a kick. If the Prince had any complaints whilst onboard it was about the reception of the World Service quite understandable when you see the array of aerials, and three masts which also doubled up as antennas. As the Prince has agreed to draw the Yacht's company raffle on the Foc'sle the communications department 'Ivy and Grobbler' in particular rigged him a voice activated receiver. In truth it was just a chair with a Commander's hat and a set of headphones suspended over the seat, so the Prince could sit straight down and slip his head into the hat and headphones without touching them. With a two way radio controlled from the Bridge, and a cassette recorder the Prince sat down; it was all systems go. Upon the command of 'World Service' came the same theme tune fading in and out that the Prince had complained about in the first place. With this prank out of the way it was time for the much anticipated Raffle.

Prizes had been kept under wraps and the Prince had kindly donated a pen and some cuff links to swell what was advertised as 'Honest

Bo's raffle'. There were a few puzzled faces in the crowd that day including the Prince when the prizes were finally revealed in all their glory. A 12 inch colour portable television, a couple of painted Chinese eggs in cases complete with insect infestation, a pen and a set of cuff links. Not exactly the bounteous fare we had been expecting at all, and anyone with five pounds worth of tickets had the right to be a bit miffed. Bo took a lot of flak on the way home from some disappointed punters, but stuck to his guns and blamed poor ticket sales. The Royal Middle East tour rolled on with the Princess leaving us on Masirah Island, but the Prince staying on to transit the Suez canal. Unlike our previous journey through the canal where the Egyptian Air Force was overhead, and the RAF took over in the Mediterranean, Colonel Gadaffi was keeping his head down, so the wooden beach was in bounds for sunbathing, when the transit had been completed. The only talk onboard at this time was the 'Chatty Raffle' as it became known, and of course the forthcoming refit in Plymouth. It would appear that Britannia was refitting in Plymouth as part of a No Strike agreement between what was now Devonport Management Ltd, and the previously employed Dockyard workers. We were a bargaining pawn in a much larger game of political chess, Yachtsmen's futures didn't enter into it, for some the Yacht had been their whole career, to me it was just a chapter, but I still doubted I was making the right decision in leaving.

Britannia had gone into meltdown, and was planning a complete De-store of all departments. The Stores Department was packing away as much as possible to make the job easier when we got back to Portsmouth. Departments were getting rid of their 'Come In Handies' that had been kept for years, to such a point that the Engineer's Workshop was destored by way of the bathroom scuttle, by a couple of over enthusiastic Stokers.

Arriving back in UK, we had a couple of weeks to complete refit preparations, a convoy of four ton army wagon's lined the jetty and half the Household Cavalry ensured that getting anything shore side that belonged to the Palace, disappeared very quickly. Royal furniture and artefacts went to Windsor castle, whilst anything belonging to the Navy went ashore to HMS Excellent on Whale Island. The only thing remaining onboard now in any quantity was bedding, and this we would get rid off in Plymouth.

## DEVONPORT REFIT 1987

Morale was at its lowest, the thought of spending the best part of a year in HMS Drake barracks, and all the travelling that involved did little to please anyone. For those who were returning to general service or were leaving the Navy 'Time done' there was hope. For everyone else who remained to standby the Yacht as she went through refit, it was going to be a long hard slog. I knew I would not have to wait too long, as my draft chit to submarines would be in the post soon. Once in Devonport's hands all remaining stores went ashore very quickly as there was now no shortage of manpower, most Yachtsmen had found themselves without a job.

The Yacht's company had been allocated billets in the newly refurbished accommodation blocks these, compared to our cramped quarters onboard were luxurious, so no complaints from anyone there. Five man cabins, showers and toilets just down the hallway and a choice of two bars on the lower floors, who could ask for more. Within a couple of weeks everyone had settled down to the routine of showing their faces onboard in the morning, and then disappearing for the rest of the day. Jake liked to keep his staff around him, so we spent most days in our porta-cabin drinking coffee and telling jokes, waiting for the next weekend leave to come around. Devonport didn't know what to do with us and to be quite honest neither did the Yacht. Over the next few months people would be sent on different qualifying courses, including Dinger who was on Petty Officer qualifying course.

I had volunteered for a parachute course, although what good an aquatic parachuting Storeman was to the Yacht was irrelevant. Leaving the Yacht looking like a rusty Russian trawler, paint stripped down to bare metal and all electrical cable stripped out of the Royal Apartments, twelve of us made our way to Dunkerswell airfield. I wouldn't have missed it for the world, and apart from the weather which stopped us from making jumps on a daily basis, a good time was had by all. Apart from Spick that is, who couldn't reach his control toggles and instead of hitting the landing zone went in the other direction for a couple of miles, Land Rover in hot pursuit. The week was over too quickly and it was back to the Yacht, where we all felt the refit wasn't going as bad as everybody thought it was going to be, plenty of time off and even the train journeys weren't that bad.

Back onboard I was collared straight away by Jake, who wanted a quiet word. Would I be prepared to stay onboard Britannia, one of the volunteer replacements had withdrawn, it was a no brainer, and now all I had to do was tell Kay. The decision to stay with Britannia pleased Jake, Kay and myself, although I would still have to join HMS Dolphin submarine training school in Gosport for a three month period, what could be better.

Exactly how many weddings I attended in 1987 I forget, but with a programme set in concrete unable to change, it was a few, including my own. My first wife had divorced me in Canada where she lived, which meant Kay and I could finally tie the knot. A very quiet affair with only us and our witness in Ramsgate registry Office, we couldn't have wished for a better more intimate ceremony. No honeymoon, just a bar b q and back to Britannia, where a witch hunt was taking place to find the culprit that had left a deposit on the table. Not any old table but right in the corner pocket of a brand new snooker table, on the same floor as our accommodation. We were treated as the main suspects because of our location being just around the corner from the snooker hall. The culprit was eventually found and turned out to be a submariner from the floor above, the only comments' from his mess mates being 'Was it in off the Pink? – or a straight brown'!

## BUCKINGHAM PALACE

Reporting to the side entrance of Buck House, Two Sheds, Blood Reid and I were soon installed in the Yellow Room, situated behind the balcony from where you normally see the Royals waving. We had been drawn out of the hat on board having volunteered for a week's work at the Palace. We would walk eight hours a day around a huge table collating pages for all the telephone directories of all the Royal Palaces. Mind numbing stuff but I was getting to see Kay in London every night, as we had a rented flat in Camberwell. Lunch would be taken with the palace staff, and the odd pint in the basement bar. I went home for the first three nights, but was determined to stay at least a couple of nights in the Palace, just for the Dit value if nothing else. Two Sheds and I gave the ball a bounce on the last night in a bar frequented by the lowest of the low, we guessed this might be for footman and scullery maids, but we fitted n well and the hospitality was second to none. Deciding to carry on down the road we ended up in the 'Bag of Nails' Public House on Buck House Road. We weren't out to impress, but when asked by a couple of Uptown girls what can you say. Tony had no sooner spilled the beans that we were from the Royal Yacht working in Buckingham Palace, when I fell off my bar stool, obviously something I ate had disagreed with my balance mechanism, street credibility straight down the pan. Leaving on the final day we asked if we could exit the Palace through the main entrance and across the parade ground. This being granted we strode past the guardsman who sprang smarty to attention as we approached, and must have thought we were right idiots, as we said 'Senior Service Passing'. Returning to Britannia, it was an endless round of temporary goodbyes, several leaving runs in ale houses surrounding Plymouth dockyard, before finally getting a discharge note and train ticket with a weekend pass thrown in.

## HMS DOLPHIN

I felt sorry for everyone else in the classroom that first day – it turned out I was the only volunteer. All the rest had been drafted from surface ships, or were straight from basic training. I sat at my desk with a draft chit in front of me, and a smug smile stretching from ear to ear. Five minutes later I was being asked to go to the Main Naval Store, and report to 'Gus the Stores PO in charge. I hadn't even settled in before 'Gus' informed that he and his wife had lost a child quite recently ,and that if possible he would like to get home as often as possible. A solution acceptable to the both of us was thrashed out. Gus would turn up every morning and disappear as soon as he wouldn't be missed, and I would get a very long weekend, but most of all every weekend! Thursday night would involve packing my car, driving around to Portsmouth, and find free parking as close to HMS Vernon as possible. Friday morning would see me showing my face in as many of the Stores Offices as possible, changing into civvies in the store, before leaving by the back door and getting the dockyard ferry across to my car, I could be home by 1300 on a good day. This worked a treat and the weeks whizzed by almost without incident. On a rainy morning, head down not looking were I was going, I turned a corner and head butted some scaffolding. I was knocked out cold. The blood made it look worse than it was, spreading as it was across my face with the aid of the rain, but there was no getting away from the fact that I had got concussion. Had I not been going back to Britannia, there was a very good chance I would not have been able to stay with submarines. It would have been back to general service with all the bells, buzzers, whistles and bull that went with it.

## SNAPS

October soon came around and I was to join Britannia as she completed her Sea Trials in the channel. Finally after a couple of hours waiting on the jetty I got a lift on a dockyard tender that that was bringing off Dockyard staff. I made my way up the accommodation ladder to be met by Norrie, 'Dump your Kit in the Barracks and I'll catch you later – I know where you'll be' was all he said, and he wasn't wrong, I was gasping for a beer. A couple of faces had changed since I was last in the Unwinding Room, but I knew most of them, and it felt like I had come home. One of the guy's introduced to me said he knew me from my time with him in the seventies onboard HMS Endurance. At the time he had been a stoker, and upon leaving had joined Britannia, but had since changed branches and was now relieving Shiner as the Yacht's official photographer. It was clear Matt and I would get on great, and as Dinger was now stuffing his Pussers grip with bottled Guinness and preparing to leave the Yacht, I would be seriously in need of a run ashore oppo.

My fondest memory of Endurance was about a particular incident that happened on our way to Antarctica. The stokers had the habit during the Middle watch, of sneaking into the dining hall and heating their cans of beans and sausages they had bought from the Naafi, on the top of the bread toasters. Stocks of toaster elements were depleting at an alarming rate, not a problem when at home but thousands of miles away and at sea, the threat of no toasters in the morning could cause enough discontent for a mutiny. Not from the consumers, but the chefs!  They would have to produce toast from underneath the grills, a very time consuming process when you're doing eggs to order and the basics preparations for lunch.  When threatened with this prospect, one chef responded with 'toast, eggs, lunch I can do the lot, just stick a squeegee up my a@se and I'll scrub out at the same time'. Once Baked Bean juice had been discovered in the bottom of the toasters the cause would be known, but the culprits not found.  The Captain decided to clear lower deck and lay down the law, anybody found wiring down the handle on the toaster so it couldn't cut out, and placing their tins upon it would get 'Nines'. Before the Skipper could get back to his cabin, someone had written a note and stuck it to his door saying 'BEANS MEANS NINES'

No one could have beaten the Skipper back to his cabin, so Ted his Steward was in the frame, but always denied it.  Clear lower deck seemed to have the required effect as an alternative heat source was found for the midnight snacks and usage of elements dropped dramatically; just as well as I didn't want to be the one to tell the chef that his squeegee was ready for collection from the main naval store.

## CIRCUMNAVIGATION 1988

With Britannia looking as good as she has ever done, the task was now to get her ready for sea.  All but the very last fresh provisions were aboard, and the task of checking most of the new equipment fitted during the last ten months had been completed during our journey round to Portsmouth. We had been fitted with a new gyro compass, this one in a box about a foot square, to replace our old one that looked like a Webber bar B Q kettle and took up most of the compartment that housed it. Like most things when they left Britannia, they were destined for a museum, and not before time, the old compass would often set off alarms when its mercury pots were running low, something I would attend to as the gyro compartment had been next to the Clothing Store. We would have a compass swing around a buoy to calibrate the new small gyro compass, and be ready for our sailing date of 6$^{th}$ January. Our deployment of six months was going to take us west about, through the Panama Canal and across the Pacific, all places I had never visited so far in my naval career. As always the tasks of getting Britannia up to Royal Duty standard started as soon as we left the jetty.

After 18 months of looking after the Yacht's uniform needs, I had been given a job change to the Main Naval Store, a task I relished but knew I had a lot of hard work ahead of me to get it up to scratch. The deck needed completely chipping back with air driven needle gun and repainting, all the storage drawers needed relining and polishing, and there were a couple of hundred of them. I would do the noisy bit of chipping in the forenoon and the quieter tasks in the afternoons not wanting to keep the watch keepers in the for'ard mess above me awake. These jobs although mundane would pass the time, and that was something we were going to have a lot of.

## MORNING COLOURS

Alongside in St Georges Bermuda for four days was a welcome diversion, plenty of dark and stormies (rum and ginger beer) and of course sunshine. For the band it was the same old routine, rehearsals in the morning and if they could find a gig, band concert in the evening ashore, other commitments (i.e. Wardroom Duty) permitting. It wasn't just the Yachtie's that enjoyed the music; it went down well with the locals where ever we went.

Morning colours were always accompanied by a few military tunes, and of course The National Anthem, but for one poor soul it was too much. During a lapse in the music all that could be heard was a voice booming 'Shut that @!*!@n! Racket up'. One local had just earned himself a home visit from the Police and the Naval Attaché. Either the music improved over the next couple of days or he was in jail for telling the band to do something - we told them every day. We sailed to Barbados for a visit by Prince Philip and Princess Margaret, before moving down for our transit of the Panama Canal, stopping for fuel and a rugby game against Rodman Naval Base. Like most games played ashore against much stronger opposition, we would normally lose the first and second halves, but we always won the third half in the clubhouse.

## DURASSIC PARK

Situated for'ard of the Unwinding room on the Port side was the smallest of Mess decks on Britannia. With several changes over the years to the Unwinding room, what was once part of the bar area, had become a mess deck for foreign contingent sailors. The Cox'n had decided that this would now house six volunteers from the Yacht's company, so that the contingent could take their places in the Mess decks proper. It was a place for volunteers as being so far for'ard it was very uncomfortable in a rough sea, and there wasn't room for a cat, never mind swinging it. About eight feet square it housed, six bunks, six lockers, a coat rack and a pole about four feet in diameter that housed the anchor cable. I jumped at the chance to get out of the After Mess, which I rarely spent any time in, mostly because the television and video were always on. Mess deck games like 'Uckers' and cards had given way to the 'One Eyed Idiots Lantern'.
The Annexe as the mess was known had no television, no radio and most of all no phone. If someone wanted you they had to find you personally, or leave messages all over the Yacht for you to find them – Bliss. My messmates would be Dave (Mother hen), Bluey, Derek, Pony and one from the Band. Although there was only one scuttle in the bulkhead to be polished it presented its own problems. Mother

Hen was far too large, Derek too rotund, Blue too tall and the Bandie too lazy, it always fell to Pony and myself or it didn't get cleaned, which was almost as bad as cleaning it and having a scuttle run (trail of Brasso down the Yacht's side, a hanging offence)!.

Another consideration was the noise from the Unwinding room itself, which was in use one way or another from 0700 until last one out at night. As the six of us were known as 'Bar Flies' a term used for all those that could be found in the Unwinding Room, mostly because like the Royal Marines Band they had nowhere else to go when off duty, not all mess decks had the luxury of a sitting out area, or mess square as it was known. If there was noise coming out of the bar, it was a sure bet we were making some of it.

## PACIFIC AND BEYOND

To finally make the gateway to the west, was to me mesmerizing, I had never seen the likes of it before or ever again. It made the Suez in comparison look like the Grand Union Canal. This was engineering of a vast scale. The Yacht would be controlled during her transit tethered to four trains, one on each corner, as the front ones pulled on their steel cables the after ones would pay out vice versa as required. It was fascinating to watch, and I spent most of the transit on the upper deck, the main store long having been locked under a water tight hatch, as it was below the water line.

Our first Royal Duty was to be low key with the Duke of Edinburgh in the Galapagos Island, and it was made quite clear that if you were not required onboard, you were to get ashore at every opportunity. For day workers like myself this was easy task, and on a daily basis I could be found carrying camera equipment for Snaps, who was taking pictures at such a rate, I felt sure we would run out of film. For ten days we were swimming with penguins, walking probably in the footsteps of Darwin. The photographic opportunities were fantastic and Matt made sure he was getting a shot of everything. We would spend most of the day ashore, and the evenings and half the night onboard printing photographs to satisfy the needs of the Yacht's company. On to Los Angeles for the Duke and Duchess of York and more Sea Days, before finally making our way across the Pacific, first stop Hawaii. My days in the Main Store chipping paint of the Deck were coming to an end, much to the relief of everyone in earshot of the noisy beast; the results of all this hard work would soon be seen at our next lot of pre Royal Duty rounds by the Admiral and Commanders. With Pago Pago also behind us, our next port of call was to be 'Nuku'alofa in Tonga', and hopefully yet more time off to explore, along with Matt I was in my element.

Invites ashore had been received by the Cox'n, and as always it was names in the hat, these invites were always popular with the Lads. Only one motor boat would be required to take the twelve lucky guys across to Paradise Island for a Bar B Q in a Hotel with a display of local dancing. Our boat Cox'n was to be Mick or 'Pound For Pound' as he was known, after his constant brags that for his weight he was the strongest man onboard – smell isn't everything is it Mick!, the day was second to none, good food, a perfect Kiwi Host and ladies in grass skirts, but alas not wearing coconuts. Mick we could see was getting worried about failing light and wanted to get the motorboat back, and with a couple of volunteers we set off, with the host sending another boat to bring us back again for some evening's festivities. Once the boat was safely back I set about finding Matt, to tell him what he was missing, and before long we were all in the skiff going back to the Island yet again. Dinner was served with much banging of a hollow tree trunk, and the party continued on until the early hours. We were accommodated in grass huts within the Hotels complex, and in the early morning all mustered for the journey back.

The small skiff that carried three plus its Cox'n on the way over, now had the task of carrying fourteen back the other way. Wind and tide were both against us, and it was soon clear that we were not only making very slow headway, we would be very late reporting for duty. The Cox'n aware that he was missing a substantial number of Yachtsmen paced the upper deck, whilst keeping an eye on the vessel that was fighting to cross the reef, blissfully unaware that these were his miscreants. We did finally arrive only to be lined up along the Port side waist to incur the Coxn's wrath. 'You've not heard the last of this he shouted – now get below' Norrie could be a softie and not only did we never hear of it again, the Buffer passed Matt and myself and said 'don't worry they don't get rid of the professionals'.
With that still ringing in his ears, Matt had found out from the Admiral's driver 'Pony' that the Admiral would not be using his car that afternoon. Taking this opportunity to have a run out to photograph flying foxes, he asked if I wanted to go, not feeling as bullet proof as him when it came to people not being got rid of, I declined. At the back of my mind was also the fact that my DO might want a word or two. He actually saved my rollicking for my divisional interview, where he informed me that I had seen myself off for an Exceptional write up, not for being late in Tonga, but for the fact we had words in Barbados on the way out. I had told him in no uncertain terms what I thought of him, whilst probably under the influence of course, I'm not that brave. The punishment fitted the crime, if I was to take his advice and keep my nose clean, this would be the last of it.

### R & R

The Naval Dockyard of Garden Island in Sydney is situated in the district of Kings Cross, miles from anywhere, and the Yacht's berth was even miles further away than that. We were obviously being kept out of the way until we had a little maintenance period and a touch up on the paint work here and there. We had just come half way across the globe, so even after our time in Plymouth needed a bit of attention. This would happen without a lot of the Yachtsmen being present, as a period of R & R had been granted, and the Yachtsmen were taking full advantage of it. Guys were flying everywhere; some had family to visit in either Australia or New Zealand, but most were flying their wives out. My wife, unlike all the others that had flown out via Hong Kong on the same aircraft, was not on the jetty when Britannia berthed. She hated waving at the Yacht as it came alongside, and was always aware that even amongst the wives there was certain snobbery which she loathed. She turned up at lunchtime with her friend, our host for the next two weeks. Debbie had jumped ship and married an Aussie called Bruce, they lived in the Greek quarter. At one time she had got involved with a con man in UK who had ran up big debts on her credit card, and getting off a boat in Sydney was her way of escaping not just him but the debt as well. Sydney was set to have the worst weather they had seen for years. When it rained it rained for days, apart from one day on Bondi beach we would be confined to the shopping malls. The time passed slowly and I think even Kay was glad to be going home.

When Britannia moved from her berth in Garden Island to the liner berth at Circular Quay, Australian hospitality kicked in. It appears no one knew we had been here for a fortnight, which only added to the resentment the guys felt that had been stuck out in the back of beyond doing all the work. With a Royal Party embarked it was back to work and off to Brisbane and Newcastle. Friends of mine turned up out of the blue in Brisbane, Dave and Jo who's daughter Ava I had courted in the UK and followed to Canada, were now residents in Australia, and of course offers of hospitality were gratefully received. With further calls in Cairns for fuel and the opportunity to go white water rafting, before moving on to Darwin for our last visit before our Northbound passage. I still pinch myself today and think to myself 'Did I really get paid for doing all this'

## COBBLERS

The passage back from Australia was always going to be a long one, with just fuelling stops to break up the routine. Of all of these Cochin in India was to provide the entertainment free of charge, courtesy of the Principal Medical Officer. There appears to be nothing you cannot buy or sell in India, and most of it is available on the jetty. Souvenirs are the normal purchase, but when the PMO saw a cobbler in attendance, he thought it would be a good idea to get his 'doe skin white tropical shoes', costing over £30 when available onboard, resoled. Entrusting his shoes to a local who was sat cross legged on the jetty next to an old India radial tyre that had done a million miles, the result could have never been in doubt. Having cut a piece of tyre about an inch square, this was quickly attached to the sole of the shoe with a few stitches or rather lashings of thick twine. A crowd had already formed when the PMO returned to collect his footwear, and refused to go away until he had least paid the man for the job. Chants of 'try them on' had to be complied with, and only after he had taken a few tentative steps up and down the jetty, did the laughter increase to a mild roar. He limped so badly that someone then shouted 'With a limp like that – you really ought to see the Doctor'. This sent the crowd into further bouts of rapturous laughter, all to the bemusement of the cobbler, whom I'm sure thought he had done a first class job. A quick stop in Aden before our transit of the Suez, and a stop in Souda Bay to let off the advance leave party; these guys would have their leave and be waiting for us upon our return to UK. It's not the normal routine to carry out a Royal Duty with a quarter of the crew away, but we were to meet up with the Queen Mother in Palermo.

# OLD QUEENS

It would be all hands of all departments to the pumps for a five day Royal Duty, Her Majesty bringing out some of her own staff to help out as well. Some of the Queen Mother's staff was well known for being gay, and I believe that is the reason she employed them, meticulously clean and tidy in all their duties. It is rumoured that two of them were having a bit of a set to in one of the pantries, which must have been overheard by Herself, for its reported she had shouted out 'When you two old Queens have quite finished – This old Queen will have a Gin and Tonic' The source of this story is unknown, but I will have to admit to dining out on it a few times.

# THE REST OF 88

After two weeks leave we were preparing once again for Cowes and the following Western Isles Cruise. Of all the Royal Duties I liked these least. I wasn't a fisherman and found that when not on duty there was very little to do in the way of entertainment. Runs ashore were few and far between, so in the confines of the Unwinding Room over a few tins, plans were drawn up to produce a video show onboard. Nick Nicholson would head the cast as a reporter, with the idea of visiting as many compartments as possible, and hopefully producing a sort of 'Candid Camera' show. I would write the very bad scripts which would contain anything of a current affairs nature, along with just a load of silliness. If someone had dropped a clanger it would soon be picked up on. First we had to get Barcelona out of the way which was to be our last Royal Duty and Sea day for the year; we'd never had it so easy. If Barcelona was to hold any memories it could only be for the longest Man Ship in the Yacht's history. We had been marched out to line the Yacht's side as always in good time, so that when the Royals arrived we were all in our positions. Nearly three hours later in the dark they arrived, information was so sketchy getting to Britannia, no one wanted to make the decision to stand us all down, in case they turned the corner as we were marching off. It was also rumoured that at one point we not even going to be stood at ease in case those at the back took the order to disperse.

Our first attempt at the video show now called 'Through Your Scuttle' or TYS for short, introduced people as furniture; a sort of human Antiques Road show, even Rear Admiral Garnier had a part as a Victorian writing desk. We then visited a chef in the galley, a stoker in the engine room, and always had a sketch in the laundry. It was loved by some and loathed by others, but Nick and I would continue and try to get as many people involved over the years as we could. We persevered and by the time Britannia had finished we had filmed ashore in Brazil and every ocean of the world, featuring all our regular guests. Cordon Bluey the galley chef, the laundry crew, the odd Officer or two and had stitched up just about every member of the Yacht's company one way or another. It was either black mail – or pay back, depending on which way you looked at it.

## THREE BADGE MAN 1989

I was half expecting my DO not to recommend me for my third good conduct stripe (each one representing four years service) and probably if I had been serving on any other vessel other than Britannia, he wouldn't have. My run ins it seemed were not deemed serious enough for a break in good conduct, so on the 15th March I marched to the Commander's table to be awarded it. I was now no longer the only two badge man in the Annexe, although I assumed due to my small statue, this would make no difference as to who polished the scuttle. As three Badge men went, Britannia had more than her fair share; in years previous they had enough to line the gangway top to bottom and did, only to be told that the photo will not go in the 'Navy News' the Royal Navy monthly rag, as it gives the wrong impression. In the Annexe alone we could proudly say that between six of us we had in excess of 100 years Royal Navy Service, and at this time about 70 years of that was Royal Yacht service. That was no mean feat, just me letting the side down rather badly.

The year was a quiet one compared to the previous couple and apart from trips to Newcastle and The Channel Islands, things wouldn't change until later in the year. One planned visit to Dover in Kent pleased me as it was only twenty miles from home, not that I could have visitors onboard, but we did get a chance for families to witness Beat the Retreat. Kay and I duly arrived at the gate and I asked at what time would Yachtsmen and their wives be allowed through, 'Join the queue at the back' was his response, until I asked him for his number. 'Why he asked' – because when the Admiral asks why my family were not at the front, he will want to know the reason, and as far as I am concerned – 'Your It'! was my reply. A van was hastily sent for and I found myself explaining to the driver that I had not picked up the ladies in Dover Town square – one was my wife and the other a friend. We got to the front just in time as the gates opened and the general public came up the jetty as if taking part in a bayonet charge battle cries and all. Apart from the Band you couldn't see anything because the tide was so far out; Britannia had disappeared below the Jetty with just mast heads, verandah deck, boat deck and bridge remaining in view. I did manage to get Matt, Pony, Tom and Derek home for a couple of hours for a beer in my local but we all had to return to Dover that evening as we were sailing to Caen in France the following day. With only an overnight in Caen, Command must have thought it would have been a quiet jolly until a Yachtsman got run over and seriously injured, being left behind as we made our way back to Portsmouth. Cowes and Western

Isles were our next commitments, before we could take summer leave and prepare with more major storing for yet another Far East Deployment.

## THE DAY THE MUSIC DIED

We had sailed from Portsmouth on the 5$^{th}$ September, and as always it was straight into deep cleaning, and preparing for the Commanders and Admirals rounds which always preceded any period of Royal Duty. So it was a shock when the signal was received onboard saying that a bomb had wreaked havoc at 0825 on the 22$^{nd}$ September at the Royal Marines School of Music in Deal, Kent. The feeling onboard was disbelief and anger, the Bandies were to take it a lot harder and many a tear was shed in privacy of the traps in the 'Heads'. Not everyone on board knew someone who had lost their life that day, but all could sympathise with those that did.

### No longer with us

Musn Jones – Musn Fice – Musn Cleatheroe - Cpl Davies
Cpl Pavey – Cpl McMillan – Musn Petch- Musn Reeves
Musn Nolan – Musn Ball – Musn Simmonds (Bob)

Our concern onboard was with those left behind at home. Not all the lads were married, but like Bob some had been in relationships for years, and we wondered if their partners would be looked after. Every indication coming from Command was the no one would be left out from any Welfare that the Royal Marines could offer. In the Unwinding Room there was silence, no longer would we have 'Root Beer Rag' on a Sunday, we had truly lost our **PIANO MAN.** One and all asked to see Divisional Officers, trying to ensure that finances would be quickly sorted out for relatives. Wheels were in motion back in the UK setting up the RMSM disaster fund, onboard we were to do some fund raising of our own. The Band held a concert on the foc'sle and TYS provided the entertainment in the intermission. Nick and I acted out some sketch involving a Rocker, a tart and a dog, which was really someone wearing lots of mop heads. I also told the monologue of the Battle of Trafalgar having borrowed every long service medal from the lower deck, pinned to my tropical jacket (see front cover). How much was raised that day is unknown, but with ten pence put on each can of beer, it started the ball rolling. The Band played marvellously with wet eyes, dry lips and sore throats, for them the music never died; it paused just for the briefest of moments.

## JAKES DIARY

Arriving in Port Klang, Jake had invited me to join him ashore for a meal, which we were assured, was cheap but plentiful, by those that dined ashore the night previous. He had omitted to tell me that he had also invited my DO until later, but this could be a good time for me to bury the hatchet, and as I had already agreed to go, there was no way out. With a quick rabbit run around the shops before dining, Jake spotted what he thought was the bargain of the trip, a 1990 diary with a page for each day, all for the price of one ringet (10 pence). With the meal being consumed the talk was all of Jakes latest bargain, and it was obvious he couldn't wait to get back onboard and start filling it in with next year's programme. The following day we found Jake going through every Shortcast, Longcast and memorandum that had been published with reference to next year's Royal Yacht programme. It wasn't long before a few printing errors started to emerge. Not all of them obvious. If the standard issue diary of the Navy stated that the 31$^{st}$ of December 1990 was a Monday, you knew it would be right, no need to doubt it – so why did Jake's show it as a Friday? Many an alteration had to be made before Jake could attend a Diary meeting with the Boss with any confidence. The Royal Duty with The Queen and Duke in Malaysia, followed closely by another in Hong Kong for The Prince and Princess of Wales, ensured that everyone was kept busy, and before we knew it, we would be making the passage home again, arriving in time for Christmas. With Hong Kong and Singapore on the shopping run, we would be floating a lot lower again in the water. Those that had missed out on a dragon pot, porcelain elephants, umbrella stands or just vases for Christmas wouldn't be missing out on them this year. The jetty in Singapore was fuller than I had ever seen it before, so much so that a stores party was organised from the Unwinding Room to get it all onboard; all storerooms were bursting again.

My thoughts at this time were on the beginning of next year when I was meant to be attending Petty Officers professional qualifying course, but Jake had concerns about the future programme and I was persuaded to postpone until a more suitable time in 1991. This was okay, but the pressure would be on from day one, if I were to fail, it would set me back 5 years on the advancement roster, and I would have to re-sit the exams I had taken in 1986. Putting all this to the back of my mind became easier with the advent of all the thank you parties to attend as we made our way west. Darts night in the Laundry was always a laugh, Rugby club drinks on the quarterdeck, endless call rounds to the water cooler and anything the club swinger could think of as well. Upper deck 'It's a Knockout' was always the favourite, along with Deck Hockey which I didn't play, as it was far too brutal. As a spectator sport Volley Ball was always a good one, with the ball encased in a net and strung with a line to the top of the net. Ninety nine times out of a hundred the line held as the ball went over the Yacht's side, on the very occasion it didn't, we didn't have a replacement ball. What must it be like to wield the power to say 'Hard a Port and rescue the ball' and have nearly five thousand tons turn full circle, whilst lowering the crash boat? I knew I should have joined as an Admiral. If one other pastime kept me busy it was cutting hair, I'd started just for mess mates in the Unwinding Room, never wanting it to escalate, as it was never a job I liked. On Britannia it was a lucrative pastime. Whilst Mitch the PO Steward would be in the electrical workshop or some other location, I had been given carte blanch to use the Unwinding Room. Charge for a haircut was one pound or three beers, most gave me a pound and then came back with a beer. At the end of each session I would have to hand back to the bar so many cans to be taken at a later time or date. The record for haircutting was the complete Royal Marine Band of thirty chaps in one sitting, I had a locker full of one pound coins, and so many beers in credit I wouldn't have to buy one for a week.

## NEGATIVE TIES 1990

With a maintenance period taking us well into the middle of February, our first port of call for the year was going to be Las Palmas. Rob who had arranged for all the families to fly out to Sydney was now arranging another holiday package. Four days was hardly going to be the longest of breaks, but any winter sunshine for the families was a blessing. Matt and I had arranged for our wives Martaine and Kay to join us, and got ashore at the first opportunity. The hotel being close by it wasn't long before we were on the beach with a beer in each hand. Ted the PO electrician hadn't been ashore ten minutes before some local had it away on his tootsies with his wife's handbag. Their passports and money now belonged to someone else. Half his holiday would be taken up with the local Police. The necktie problem was talked about onboard, and was a very sensitive issue; any Yachtsman ashore after 1800 must wear a tie, which would see many a Yachtie legging it into a toilet wearing a soft collared shirt, and come out wearing a dress shirt and tie, no matter where we were in the world, but as we were on holiday do we wear them or do we not? The general consensus was 'No Way' the ladies at this time were sick of hearing about ties.  Seeing Connie the New Buffer arm in arm with his wife on the first night, dressed only in his shorts and flip flops, confirmed we were in the clear.  The following evening 'Connie' was dressed overall, shirt, tie, slacks and no smile. It appeared that a compromise had been reached, Senior Yachtsmen would comply with 'Royal Yacht Standing Orders dress policy', Yachtsmen would be allowed to 'Stand Easy' and relax ties. Matt and I like all the other Yachtsmen just kept our heads down, and stayed out of the way hoping no one would notice us.

## WEST AFRICA

Passing through Freetown and Abidjan we arrived at Lagos to complete a Royal Duty with The Prince and Princess of Wales.  Runs ashore were at a minimum as there was nowhere to go but the German Seaman's mission, fine for a swim and a day time beer but the evenings would see everyone staying onboard.  Work towards the latest set of Admiral's rounds had all been done, I had only one job to complete before the Royals arrived and that was to dispose of any unserviceable stores.  Items that could not be repaired or that were of no resale or scrap value were written off by the Supply Officer and normally just thrown into a skip. Here all our rubbish was being gone through by the locals, and they were keeping everything right down to the brown paper sacks the rubbish was in.  Maritime law prohibited the routine of throwing things over the side, so clutching an old clock, two gauges and a one legged ironing board, I made my way off the gangway towards the direction of a forty five gallon oil drum being used as a dustbin, when I was stopped by a Nigerian sailor who should have been guarding the jetty. 'Are you going to ditch that'?  he said in the deepest African voice I'd ever heard. 'Yes I replied'- 'Give it to me' he said and took the ironing board with its one leg. He stood the rest of his four hour shift at the bottom of the gangway, dressed in his best white uniform clutching his prize to his chest like a Zulu shield. Over the next few hours people made excuses to go and see the sailor on the jetty, with the consensus being that he probably didn't own an iron, judging by the creases in his attire, and would probably stay until I took an iron ashore, I never did – sorry.

The Prince and Princess were to have a walk round and meet the crew, date and time set and the programme produced. All mustered at our allotted stations to meet the Royal couple, when the for'ard air conditioning plant decided to take a few hours rest. The result being the temperature inside the for'ard end of Britannia was becoming very quickly unbearable. New places to meet and greet were quickly sorted out, most of them were on the upper deck, which was not without its own drawbacks. The smell from the Gulf of Guinea was interesting to say the least; I had personally seen a bloated dead animal float past the Yacht, whilst keeping an outboard sentry watch on the upper deck that very morning. The view on the jetty had been better but only visible from the Quarterdeck, a standpipe being used by the local ladies as a shower, what was going to be a boring watch turned into a very interesting one. Both the Prince and Princess brushed aside the discomforts and met as many Yachtsmen as possible, although the smell was mentioned more than once. The Princess asked about the Unwinding Room which she referred to as the smoky place where she had once played the piano. I had been onboard for over four years and had never heard of the Princess dropping in for a quick pint, never mind a tinkle on the ivories, so it must have been on her honeymoon. Towards the end of the Royal Duty, I was helping Snaps on the verandah deck take down all his equipment after an official photograph, when The Princess remarked what a pleasant evening it was. Bucking up courage I asked if she ever got upset about what the press write about her boys; she replied

'I'm not raising bloody ballerinas' smiling. With only quick calls in Douala, Freetown and Las Palmas for fuel, we would head back to Portsmouth, and the essential job of maintenance on one of our boilers could commence. We would be in dry dock for a month, just enough time to rectify all the defects before our next planned visit to Iceland, a review of the Cunard Fleet in the channel, also a visit to London.

## HAPPY BIRTHDAY

Being on full view in the Pool of London, moored by Tower Bridge and adjacent to HMS Belfast, which had HMS Broadsword alongside her was very special indeed. The atmosphere and hospitality ashore was second to none, and we were centre stage having Her Majesty the Queen Mother onboard for her 90th Birthday. Snaps had a plan to get as many photographs for the firework spectacular as possible, and whilst he would be covering Britannia from the Dockside, I was despatched to No1 London Bridge to cover all three ships and London Bridge. If I have any failings with cameras, it has always been not to get the picture in focus. I must have got it right on this occasion as Matt thought I had taken a good enough photograph to be put into a competition; it came third, but best of all, it was taken up for the cover of the reception programme for the centenary of Tower Bridge, to be held onboard in 1994. My claim to fame this day is that it is my photo that was used, and my name in the programme – not Matt's, sorry mate.

## GOODBYE SIR

Rear Admiral Garnier was set to hand over command to the new Incoming Flag Officer, Rear Admiral Woodard in September. We would all feel his loss, Big John was always known as a gentleman, the kind of Officer that if you passed him in the dockyard whilst he was wearing his civvies would raise his hat to you in return for a salute. It was a sad day when three well meant cheers went up from the Yacht's side, where all serving Yachtsmen had gathered to bid him a final goodbye. Matt again would score points by presenting him with an aerial photograph of his house as a farewell gift, and the Unwinding Room gave him the same but taken from a different angle. With friends in the right places like the Fleet Air Arm, these were easy to obtain. He would also be the first Flag Officer to be presented with his 'Pint Glass' which was normally housed behind the bar in the Unwinding Room, engraved and exclusively reserved for the Flag Officer's use. Her Majesty knighted him onboard Britannia before he departed; we believe that he may have been the only person to be knighted at sea since Raleigh or Drake.

We sailed for South America within a few days of the changeover of command, and lots of hard work went in getting Britannia as shiny as she had ever been for the Admirals first set of pre Royal Duty rounds. The new Admiral was definitely hands on, and made himself self known throughout Britannia very quickly, with constant visits to all departments. We arrived in Bridgetown for the Princess Royal and everything seemed to be going smoothly when what seemed like an explosion could be heard from stem to stern. Everybody thought that we had been bombed, but were proved to be wrong when it was discovered that a steam driven plate heater in the Royal Servery had decided to give up the ghost. Clive Hobbs became the luckiest Royal Steward onboard, as he had been arranging flowers on it just minutes before. He missed having his head taken off at the neck by seconds, the working surface of the heater rose about four feet crushing the fan trunking in the deck head above. The Shipwrights Alan and John would have their work cut out repairing not only the heater but the deck head as well. We proceeded on to Rio for a Sea Day, and our visit almost went without incident, apart from Derek Bond the PO Steward who had taken himself off to Copacabana beach for a swim whilst off duty, only to find when he returned to his towel that the locals had nicked all his clothes. He would have to make it back to Britannia wearing only his swimming shorts, luckily it was before 1800 and he wouldn't be done for not wearing a tie. Our journey would take in Fortaleza, which got nicknamed Fortasleazer for the bars and beaches were teaming with ladies of the night. It proved to be a popular run ashore, but three days of sun and sand is enough for anyone; time to go home.

## NOMADS

Ashore with Derek, Matt and the new Caterer's Assistant Andy we ended up in the Sheraton Hotel in Funchal playing darts of all things. We were approached by a group of Americans celebrating thanksgiving, who had mistaken us for airline pilots because of our ties and accents. Correcting their mistake by showing them Britannia that was visible from the window, an invite to join them on the 11th floor was soon in the offering. The Nomads as they insisted on calling themselves we discovered, were quite an elite holiday group that owned their own aircraft. Following them up in the lift with our arms full of Gin, Vodka, Whisky and Rum and all the mixers, we were in for a very long night. We had not been there half an hour when I noticed Andy climbing over the balcony; why was not exactly clear at this point. Grabbing hold of Matt, we secured a hold on each arm and proceeded to hoist him back onto firmer ground. Feeling very embarrassed Andy was well and truly given a dressing down not just from us but the Nomads as well. Eleven floors up and a belly full of beer he could have easily killed himself if I had not noticed his strange exit. This we discovered was his way of getting attention; well he got that and almost a lot more. The night drew to a close but not before each of us got the names of four people, and invited them onboard as our guests the following day. The walk back to Britannia was only about half a mile through the docks, but having a little stagger on I took a tumble and ended up on my back. Lying on the ground with my feet in the air, I remarked that I thought I might have been hit by a sniper. With much laughter we continued keeping our eyes on the rooftops, just in case I should suffer the same fate again.

Twelve Nomads turned up the following day, and between the three of us were given the full tour, before proceeding down to the Unwinding room for refreshments. There were a few baggy heads between them, but as soon as some Courage Sparkling Bitter was administered they were back on an even keel. One of the ladies I had been showing round, confided in me that she had been recently widowed and made it quite clear she was looking for someone new in her life. Making sure she knew I was married, I set about introducing her to anyone I knew to be single. She did finally click with one of the older guys and that was the last I saw of him and most importantly of her.

As we were sailing for UK the following day the pilot of the Nomad's plane suggested that as his take off slot was a couple of hours after our sailing, he might be able to arrange to overfly Britannia. Derek, Matt, Andy and I stood on the quarterdeck holding a huge White Ensign, but the airplane never arrived much to the amusement of the other Yachties, who didn't believe there was an aircraft. Our final trip of the year was to be in the Pool of London; unfortunately this was to be Matt's last voyage with us. He was due to be rated Petty Officer and for this to take effect he would have to leave his post as Snaps. There would be no more coffee in the dark room at stand easy for Derek and myself in the morning, with Matt's secret ingredient known only as developer but smelling a lot stronger, so much so, we would have to use an air freshener before opening the door - I wonder what it was!

# COLLEGE OF KNOWLEDGE 1991

I managed to attend my Father's funeral, before agreeing with Kay that my forthcoming Petty Officers qualifying course should be treated as sea time. As the course was in HMS Raleigh in Plymouth I wouldn't be coming home at weekends, allowing me to throw myself completely into my studies. I had heard that the course was quite intensive, and the failure rate was high, and with five years seniority to lose as well as face on board, I thought that ten weeks was a small price to pay for the rewards that could follow. Having travelled down the previous day to the course starting, I set about settling into my accommodation. Basic but comfortable, four bunks in the one room with television and bathroom facilities down the corridor. My three classmates Jacko, Doc, and Paul were soon to join me, and a plan for the forthcoming course was laid out. We agreed that whatever extra work was required of an evening to make sure we were all up to the same speed, would be done before supper. After that we would work on our course projects individually, and at 2000 hrs no matter how far we had or hadn't got, we would retire to the Naafi bar and discuss any problems any one was having. This worked well as we all had a lot of experience, some more than others in different fields. Between the four of us, we felt confident that there wasn't a question we couldn't answer collectively We were introduced to our instructor Keith and the nightmare began, with only four students and four corners to a classroom we were separated as far away from each other as possible. Paul and Jacko would disappear at the weekends, leaving me and Doc to put in lots of overtime and have an easier time of it. Exams were set every Thursday morning, whilst Thursday afternoons was set aside for a beer ashore with Keith whilst our papers were being marked. We would normally return to the classroom about 1600 to get the results. As a copy of all course members photographs were posted in the

My first and nearly my last run ashore – 'Nigs' no hat middle back behind Dinger in the blue shorts, Jake in red vest. S & S dept 1985

Top      - Jolly boats rescuing refugees from the beaches of Aden
Bottom  - Royal apartments turned into dormitories

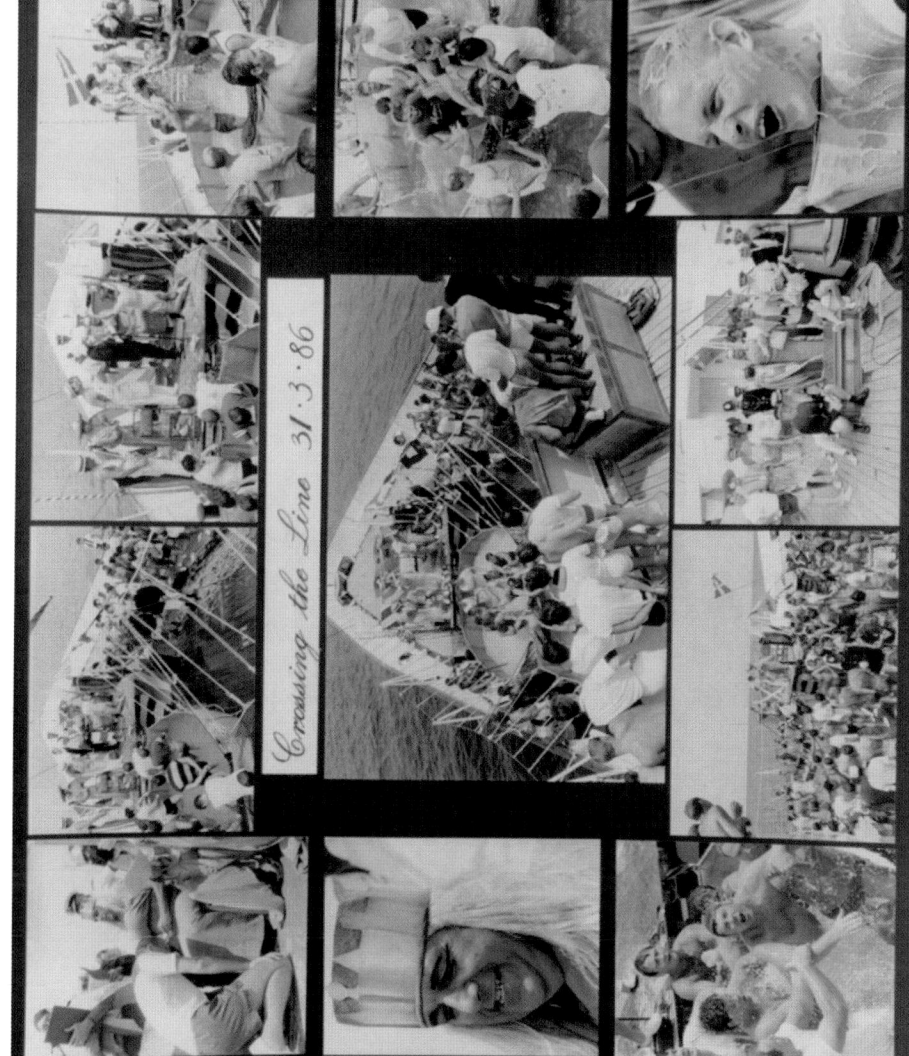

Crossing the Line 31·3·86

THE TONE DEAF'S CONCERT

Top – Royal Yacht or rusty trawler Devonport 1987
Bottom – Panama Canal transit 1988

Dress Ship Party – Port side Flag deck
Pulling flags up from the foc'sle

Top - Matt (Snaps) Rear Admiral Sir John Garnier and Myself
Bottom High, Derek, Ginge, Sandy, Ricky, Shiner, Alf, Bluey and
Mother Hen off Fortaleza

Top – Royal Yacht Rowing Team Baltimore Harbour
Bottom – Victualled Members Only – Warrant and CPO's mess

Top; At the water cooler waiting to go and entertain Her Majesty
Wee Jimmy – Myself – Nick – Harry the Back – Alf hiding
Botom: Myself – Andy – Bob – Daisy and Ladies off to the Palace

*ON HIS HORSE, WITH HIS HAWK, IN HIS HAND*

THE VILLAGE FETE PO's MESS VOLUNTEER BAND

Top – The Unwinding Room
Bottom – The Petty Officers and Sergeant's Mess

main corridor of the Supply School, anybody failing an exam would be thrown off course and a red cross struck through their photo.

This I found very harsh, but was assured that because I was on Britannia, any failure on my part would result in my face being 'snowpaked' out before I was removed from the class. The ten weeks proved to be the hardest of my career mentally, with many a phone call home to the wife predicting failure, she would have none of it and just told me to get on – you can do it. Whether it was Kay's confidence, Keith's patience, or the fact that we had all helped each other, we all got through to the final exam. The simulator as it was known, was a set of small classrooms set around a central office, where an instructor would be keeping a watchful eye on all the students. The purpose of this last practical exam was to see how you performed under pressure, not only were you expected to sort out the hundreds of problems to be found in the 'IN' tray, but different people would keep coming in and hitting you with all sorts of problems, all to be attended to with efficiency and of course courtesy. If the Instructor in the Goldfish bowl saw that you were getting flustered he would pile even more pressure on, it really was a case of 'Keep Calm and Carry On'.
These final exams were taking place on a Saturday as the simulator had been double booked, this meant that if all went well we would be finishing early during the coming week. We all passed, some with higher flying colours than others, but in my case I don't think there was any wasted effort, I found it tough. I wouldn't go back to Britannia until I had taken Easter Leave, and I truly needed the break to wind down. My first action on returning was to put in a request form to take the final part of Petty Officers qualifications, this one known as POLC, Petty Officers Leadership Course; I should have guessed that it wouldn't be granted. For whatever reason, Yacht's programme or the fact that I would still be a Killick on a PO's

course, it was turned down.  I knew that it meant I would never ever get on the course, which in turn meant further down the line, I would never ever make Chief, especially as I had just refused advancement to stay in Royal Yacht Service.

## SOUTH AMERICA 1991

During the Easter break I had been having a pint in my local The White Stag and was on my way home when an American car passed by.  Nothing too unusual about that apart from the fact you don't get many mint condition El Dorado Coupe's driving around in Pot Hole County.  I mentioned it to Kay on my return and thought no more of it.  We sailed for sunnier climes cleaning polishing and generally getting up to Yacht standard, when I was called to the Coxn's office. Norrie had finally handed over the reins to Roy Tatlow some time before, but to be called to his office was still daunting. 'Kent Police want a word with you' he said – 'if you're in trouble Your Off'!
I had phoned home from our last port of call and been told there had been a murder in the village of Monkton, Police had gone door to door asking for information about an American car, Kay of course told them I'd seen it.  I was given ten minutes on the satellite phone to sort things out with a very excited policeman who had found a witness. I'd had seen nothing I explained but he still wanted to fly out and interview me. I told him when we would be arriving in Dakar, and he said he would be there.  Before ringing off he said 'see you in Bangladesh' Hold on I said I'm going to Senegal, 'in that case he said I'll interview you when you get back'.  It would be July before we actually met, and I had since learned that the murder victim's partner was found with an electric fire in her bath; I was leaving this and the Police well alone.
Having got across the pond yet again, and with Admiral's rounds behind us, it was time to relax just a bit before our first period of

Royal Duty. With a quick stopover in Fortaleza, and just enough time to take a jolly boat out, it was straight into another Royal Duty. We were at the mouth of the Amazon in Belem with The Prince of Wales, then over to Miami for The Queen and Duke. I had been looking forward to Miami but I guess we had the wrong berth, for the only thing on the Jetty was 'Hooters' fast food outlet where the waitresses all wore hot pants, and also a shopping mall. I don't know if it was the chicken or the hot pants, but you couldn't squeeze another Yachtie in the place. Our berth in Tampa couldn't have been more different, right in the middle of town, and in the night life area. When the Yacht berthed, the crowds had come out in their hundreds to see Her Majesty.

It was obvious we were going to have a good run here, and I wasn't to be proved wrong. I had spotted a White Ensign flying from a balcony on the way into harbour, and thought it might be a good idea to find its owner. Enlisting the help of a taxi driver we tracked the owner down to a British Pub called 'Yeoman's Road', with a red telephone box outside on the pavement, and flag on the roof. They had liberated the Ensign from a visiting warship and hung it out every time a British ship entered port. If it was a ploy to drum up ex pat custom it worked, we would make it our base for the week. Immediately on the jetty was a club called Blueberry Hill which of an evening was a single man's paradise. I had never seen so many Yachtsmen wanting to get ashore in uniform before. Ahead of us was a private yacht called Misty Blue owned by a very nice couple who made half the Yacht's company very welcome over the course of the next week. If any event is worthy of note, it must be for the courage of a couple I had met on the Jetty, and the outstanding contribution made to their tour of Britannia by Alf and Bluey.

A couple (John in a wheelchair) were dining in view of Britannia, watching as an endless stream of civilian guests was coming down the gangway, having had a tour and a few beers. 'How did they get onboard' John asked; 'they were invited' I said, would you like to be my guests tomorrow. He glanced at his own legs and said only one word 'impossible'. Don't worry about that I said, just meet me on the Jetty at 1600 tomorrow, and we'll get you sorted – it was like inviting Cinderella to the ball.

When John and wife turned up they didn't have a clue what to expect. I had enrolled Alf and Bluey, being about the same size, to manhandle him around the Yacht for the full tour. John would have to negotiate the ladders himself, which he did by bouncing himself either up or down on his bottom. The tour normally takes about an hour, depending on how interested your guests were, and how many questions they asked. Our tour took two hours and ten minutes, before we got to the Unwinding Room, only twenty minutes and they would have to go. The Cox'n seeing what had been done, extended our bar time for another hour for this couple so they could relax. With all the other guests gone, the Unwinding Room became the venue for an impromptu guitar recital. John had a voice and the guitar skills to match. Gifts started to arrive in the form of a Zippo lighter from one Yachtie, a photograph of the Yacht from another, and so many beers it was obvious he would not be able to drink them all. Alf and Bluey would have to help him out, and they deserved as many beers as they could manage for their efforts. On leaving the Yacht John's wheelchair was waiting at the bottom of the gangway; the Quartermaster having towelled off the seat so it was dry after a rain shower. Lowering himself into his chariot he gave a groan and explained that he may have left a few layers of skin on every rung of every ladder, he had just previously been up or down. 'It was worth it' he said as we finished the day with a beer and a meal on the jetty where we had only met the day previously. John just kept looking at Britannia in disbelief, with the icing on the cake being when the bill came for the meal, they were expecting, and quite insistent on paying for us, but after such a good day it would have been cheap to allow that, so we had a whip round and treated them - priceless.

## CUBAN RESCUE

Certainly the bridge watch keepers didn't see him, if there was anybody on the foc'sle they didn't see him, in fact the only reason this chap is alive today, is that a sailor who was working on his boat did see him, and by this time he was half way down the Yacht's side. Using a polystyrene packing crate from a domestic fridge as a boat, and a paddle from a child's dingy as main propulsion – here was one desperate man. With the Gulf of Mexico behind him, he would have been doomed in the Atlantic, but for that one Sailor's sharp eyes. Getting both man and makeshift boat onboard, his immediate problems of survival was over, it was now down to Andy and Eric, and for them their problems were just starting. He had been at sea for quite a while (at least a week) and was badly dehydrated and seriously undernourished. No time was wasted by the PMO and his team in getting fluids back into 'Fidel' as he was now being called below decks. Our course was altered to make our way back to Miami, although I don't think he would have put up any fight if we had decided to bring him back to the UK with us. Overnight he improved dramatically, certainly well enough to walk and dress himself in a full chef's white outfit, resplendent with matching plimsolls. Helicopters from every news station in America were flying overhead, cameramen hanging out of every doorway trying to get film of the individual as we transferred him to a coastguard vessel just outside the harbour entrance. Dressed in all his white finery 'Fidel' was transferred along with his polystyrene boat, which he refused to leave behind. I expect today it is his prize possession, although he did leave the paddle behind, which somehow made its way down to the Unwinding Room, and was quickly screwed to the bulkhead, should someone ask for it back.

On our journey home we were two sailors short, as these had missed the Yacht sailing from Miami. They had stayed ashore all night in a hotel for an evening's R & R, and although they had put down for an early morning call this failed to materialize. Finally catching up to the Yacht in Tampa armed with sworn affidavits to this effect they were not cut any slack, their fate was sealed. Not their fault, but on the Yacht that didn't carry any weight, so Cliff and his side kick who hadn't been onboard that long, but both stalwart Yachties were only lucky in one way, and that was that I believe they got military flights home, thus saving them having to spend their own hard earned cash. It sent a very strong message around the Yacht – be there or miss it. We stopped at Lisbon for a quick Sea Day, before arriving off Cornwall, and were boarded by Customs Officers. This was Rear Admirals Woodard's idea; he would clear customs and get off in Falmouth, being a native of the West Country, leaving the rest of the Yacht to clear customs as we made our way up the Channel. This proved to be very popular with both the Commander and the crew, he got to play Skipper for the Night, and the Yachtsmen could clear customs in an orderly fashion. Previously Customs embarked at Outer Spit Buoy outside of Portsmouth, and all leave was delayed until all Yachtsmen had been well and truly done by Customs (and I mean well and truly done) – Nice one Sir!

# SOME BUGGERS NICKED MY UMBRELLA

With a quick trip to Milford Haven and the ever customary Cowes regatta ticked off, it was once again off to the Western Isles of Scotland.  By now even I was becoming immune to this annual drag and would throw myself into any beach party or stroll that was on offer. Calls ashore were often made by Her Majesty on the way up the coast, and as it was normally raining, the Umbrella Party was put on permanent standby to see the Royal Party onto the Barge.  On one such occasion I had again drawn the short straw, only to find that the umbrellas were not in their usual place of the Royal Servery. Many a Royal steward was despatched to search every location that they possibly could be. Finally being discovered in the Royal Charthouse, which was located three decks above and a good run from my location. I would have to make haste or be late for Her Majesty's departure, not a position I wanted to put myself or my team mates in, especially as the Commander was looking none too pleased.

 No one told me Her Majesty was taking afternoon tea in there, and had been using the umbrellas on the Royal Bridge.  Looking in I could see the umbrellas hanging up all in a line on the rail and just dashed in and grabbed the lot, only to turn and face a very astonished and very close Monarch – I ran. I heard later from the Admirals Steward 'Eric' that Her Majesty had said to the Admiral 'Some Bugger just stole my umbrella', with the Admirals reply being 'No Ma'am – The Bastard just stole your umbrella'! True or not, I again would have a Royal tale to dine out on for many a year.  I was just very glad that the only time I would hear of this again onboard would be in the Mess, and not on the Commander's Table.

A very relaxed Royal Walk round by the Duchess of York, found both Admiral and Yachtsmen in the Unwinding Room.  Making herself comfortable the Duchess asked if anyone knew a joke.  I told one of the cleanest I knew, if not the cleanest.  Whereupon she started to tell the tale of Snow White and the Seven Dwarfs. Rather a long winded joke about Dopey and a Dwarf Nun possibly having an affair. The punch line was worth the wait, when The Duchess did no more than jumped to feet and pranced around the room on tip toe to deliver it. The Admirals jaw dropped and you could have heard a pin drop! Turning to the Duchess the Admiral said 'Ma'am do you know what monkeys and acid rain have in common' – the Duchess replied 'No Admiral, pray tell'– and he did, the Navy were back in the lead by one to nil.

After some much deserved summer leave with our families, we would once again find ourselves in the Pool of London for the quickest of Royal Duties, before returning to Portsmouth, with just enough time to top up with stores. Then it was bows west once again for visits into Montreal and Toronto with The Prince and The Princess of Wales. Not the busiest of years by Britannia's standards but we had still clocked up over 25,000 miles.

## FIREARMS AND FLAIRED TROUSERS

1991 certainly seemed to be the year for shore side training of one sort or another. Lots of us had been swimming wearing full immersion suits undergoing sea survival training in Horsea Lake, not exactly recommended when the temperatures are in single figures. No sooner had we got dry it was fire fighting training on Horsea Island itself, where at least the flames were warmer than the water. Response force training followed very quickly on Whale Island. It appears all the Yacht's company were out of date for one course or another. Most courses would be using shore side instructors, but for some reason it was decided that our own Sergeant Gaz Rowley (known to most as the angry gooseberry, because of his lack of hair and short temper) would take charge of the firearms side of the response force training. Teaching about thirty Yachties at a time,

Gaz's first task was to teach the uninterested how to put the rifle sling on the standard issue 5.56mm SA80 rifle. If any qualification would have given any sailor an advantage it would have been an 'A' level in Origami. When installed on the rifle, the sling was a thing of wonderment allowing the user to sling the rifle across his back, chest and even just to hang it by his side. It was the put part A into part B whilst allowing C to run around and back through D that confused us. Lots of us lost it big time, none more so than Gaz whose patience had long since run out. After many hours of instruction we finally got it, and to the Sgt's amazement we could strip down our weapons and also put them back together without any bits left over, sling in the right place as well.

Putting our few days learning into practise would take place on HMS Kent, an old destroyer, berthed at Whale Island and used for training on a daily basis. We were taught how to check compartments for intruders, whole ship search techniques and most importantly how to challenge someone forcefully. 'HALT NAVY OR I FIRE' Gaz would shout at the top of his already threatening voice, making us all jump. We would go on and practise this many times over but never to his satisfaction. One by one we would stand up shouting at the top of our voices trying to look as menacing as possible. Things were getting better until it came to the turn of AB Dave Avis; 'Gaz' – he said 'it's alright for you, looking the part in your combat gear, but how am I to look menacing I'm wearing flairs'. It was like pulling the pin out of a grenade. He soon got over it and we moved on to the hostage rescue scenario, where one of the search team is taken by the intruders. Our team of four was searching the Burma Road, when out of nowhere came an intruder and took Harry Neilson known as 'Harry the Back' by surprise. Quick as a flash Harry was grabbed by the throat and held against a bulkhead, with his assailant between him and us. All Harry could shout was 'shoot me – shoot me, save the ship'. I hate to see a grown man cry, but I swear Gaz was close to it at this point.


## PROMOTION AND MEDAL 1992

Jake's decision to leave Britannia must have been the hardest one he ever had to make. For whatever his reasons, it wasn't to stand aside and let me get my promotion, something I had turned down a year previous, electing to stay in Royal Yacht service. He was due to leave us in March, but had so many courses to attend before joining his next establishment, we would see very little of him over the next three months. As our extended support period started, it was clear that I would take over with a baptism of fire. I'd only just learnt to swim, and here I was in the deep end. Britannia would be going into dry dock which meant all weapons and ammunition along with pyrotechnics would have to be landed, along with inflammable materials and all fuels. From the moment we got back from Canada we would hit the ground running. Thankfully well prepared for the forthcoming maintenance period and with the staff that I would inherit from Jake, and one to replace myself, we had the immediate programme nailed down. All technical departments on our previous deployment had been pointed at me if they had a query of any sort; Jake was on a very long run down period. My Divisional Officer would accompany me to the Commander's table this one last time, as I was to be rated Petty Officer. I expected some cutting remark to be made when he represented me to the Commander, but he just said 'Highly Recommended, he has after all just taken Britannia through this period as a Petty Officer in all but Rank'. As I walked away from the table he invited me in for a beer in the Warrant Officers and Chiefs mess at lunch time to celebrate, it was the first of very many invites to follow over the years. Just two days after putting on PO's uniform I found myself in the Admiral's cabin, being awarded the Long Service Medal. It would be my turn to invite Rob into my Mess to celebrate; along with the Deputy Supply Officer 'Steve Woolley' it would cost a fortune. I must have heard the saying 'Medals are like piles a hundred times that lunch time'. I knew everyone would get one.

In the PO's mess if you were buying the beer for all the mess, you would turn on a miniature diver's helmet light and place it on the bar. All the time the light is on, you're in the chair as far as the bar bill is concerned. It had been known in the past for someone to turn the light on and fall asleep in one of the armchairs forgetting to turn it off, waking up to a very, very large bill.

I would go home to Monkton for the weekend to celebrate with Kay, only to find in my Porch window a sign saying;

Congratulations Petty Officer Horne
If Russia invaded Poland from behind
Would Greece help?!!

My Neighbour, close friend and custodian of my shed key in my absence, Simon being the guilty party!

## THE THREE MUST HAVE BEERS

With Jake now off the Yacht's books, the job was definitely down to myself, and of course the staff. Spud, Andy and Geoff were quickly making a name for themselves amongst the Yacht's company; trouble was, it wasn't so much for their professional expertise as it was for their social exploits. If you found one of them ashore, off Royal Duty you could have a safe bet the other two would not be far behind. Spud was the senior of the three with several years of service behind him, a fact that made him my right hand man in the office. If my eyes occasionally showed the strain of an evening festivities, then Spud's were constantly glazed, followed occasionally by Andy and Geoff's. Their close friendship and what seemed a love of ale from all over the world would cause me great concern in the future, and I wouldn't have to wait long to find that out. Our first trip abroad was to be Gibraltar, a challenge to anyone who likes a drink; I feared the stores drinking team would be going for it. When Spud and Andy failed to show their faces in the office at 0800, I had a feeling of impending doom. Checking their mess deck, my greatest fears were confirmed, they had not returned from the previous nights run ashore. They were only a couple of minutes adrift, but were noticed by the gangway staff and duly logged as late in the incident book. Punishment was two days stoppage of leave each. They obviously didn't learn from their punishment, for as soon as we reached Malta, they repeated the offence. Rob was no longer my Divisional Officer but divisionally my staff came under him, and he was getting a bit miffed to say the least. I would have words with them, but it was to have little or no effect; Rob would go to the table with them on a regular occasion.

With all of Spud's failings I got on generally very well with him, and when he wanted to, could work hard whilst having you in stitches with his infectious humour. He had introduced to the stores office a map of the world, which he updated every time we called into a different port.

The key to the map being

Beer glass    - Good run ashore, plenty of ale houses
Palm tree     - Scenic run, but nothing to write home about
Blue toilet   - Dirty country and not a good run ashore
White toilet  - Absolute toilet, stay onboard in Unwinding room

As Spud placed his white toilet flag on half the known world, and beer glasses on the other half, it was easy to see that he favoured runs ashore in the USA, Canada, Australia and the Far East. If any of the Yacht's chandlers found their way down to the office to conduct business mostly with Ian the Caterer, they never mentioned the map on the wall. It could have been that they had no argument with Spud's findings, or maybe they just didn't get his humour. The Commander and Admiral obviously did, for during their frequent pre Royal Duty rounds they would pay more attention to the map discussing the wardroom reception and the Officer's run ashore rather than wiping their hands over the overheads trying to find a bit of dust that may have been missed by either Spud or myself.

## THE PETTY OFFICER'S MESS

I had an insight into life in the CPO's and PO's mess back in 1977, when I had been Acting PO on HMS Endurance. The PO's mess on Britannia was a whole new ball game. The Mess President 'Ted' known as 'Ruxbin' after the talking teddy bear, would only have to have words with me once in the first couple of weeks, and this only to remind me to keep whatever goes on in the office, stays in the office. I knew what he was saying 'Wind your neck in' the mess did not need to know how good I thought I was at my job. Message received and understood I never talked shop in the mess again, even if it was not me that brought up the subject in the first place. Generally life in the mess was quite relaxed and friendly, just as well as I didn't bring any friends into the mess with me. Unlike the Unwinding room, the senior's messes had a spirit bar, this being shut outside of bar opening hours. A far cry from life in the lower deck on a warship, where it was still three cans per man per day perhaps, and collected daily from the Naafi store. As a senior you could have three tots a day, of either Gin, Vodka, Scotch or the dreaded Navy Rum. Luckily I have never been one for the top shelf, only the odd rum maybe but being able to offer one's guests a spirit would be a nice change. Our bunk spaces known as gulches, each with six bunks and lockers surrounded the bar area, four inside the mess and one outside, with a sitting out area of four arm chairs and a table in the middle. Not quite as nice as the WO/CPO's mess, but perfectly functional. The noise at the bar would keep all but the most dedicated of sleepers awake, and the television like the after mess never seemed to be off. It was during my first couple of months in the mess that I started to dread the mail call. It appeared that I was the only one in the mess who didn't support any football team, leaving twenty nine others all supporting different teams, and after every mail drop clutching a video tape of the last game – Nightmare. They would take it in turns to play their own video tapes, until all had been exhausted.  This would normally happen in the afternoons, so I was able to escape to the office; work also became sanctuary. Everyone in the mess had a job, there was a president for this, a vice for that, social secretaries, bar managers, spirit Bosun's, I don't think any job had been overlooked.  I managed to squeeze into the social team, whose job it was to arrange social events with the Wardroom, Warrants and Chiefs but most of all The Petty Officer's Christmas Party. Life of an evening in the mess would follow a routine most weeks, with bingo and film nights, all raising money for ladies nights, mess dinners and most importantly the end of year bash always held ashore in a hotel with our wives in attendance.

Sunday lunchtimes were the biggest fundraiser providing we were at sea, where there could be no escape from the clutches of the raffle committee. Cheese and biscuits were laid on, and possibly some entertainment; you were encouraged to invite a guest in for a beer, so he could be mugged into buying raffle tickets as well.  One pound would secure three strips of raffle tickets, where you could win such goodies as 'smelly balls to put in your gym shoes, out of date diaries, old batteries' and so much other rubbish, I was embarrassed to sell the tickets, but most of all gutted I had to buy them as well'. If you were truly unlucky your guest, normally a Chief would then invite you over to his mess and you'd be mugged all over again. The WO/CPO's raffle being a much grander affair, the Chief Caterer's fruit pack (carton of juice) being an unfair advantage to start with; also the fact the Can Man 'Steve' would always provide freebies from the Naafi. Sundays were a very expensive pastime, but with thirty people in the mess and the average raffle prize being £100 at the Christmas Party, we had a lot of fund raising to do during the year to make the target. We all paid mess funds as well, something I had never had to do before; it soon became clear that living in the PO's mess came with certain financial commitments, and it was little wonder that some of the married men with families found it hard. On the odd Sunday morning during Church, the odd Gulch party would kick off. Exactly what the attraction was of standing between two rows of bunks at 1030 in the morning, with a glass in your hand is hard to define, but some of the best parties in the mess started in this manner. Known as a gulch party in our mess, but if was happening in any of the cabins (normally G) it became known as Matins'. If anything ever led into mischief on a Sunday in either mess in the afternoon, this was to blame. I have to admit to being a day worker and not keeping watches at sea, and that if there was a gulch party going on, I was normally there; I always thought it was rude to refuse an invite.

## THE PRESIDENT'S TROUSERS

Every now and again something happens to raise a smile, and in Ruxbin's case morale as well. On one of Ted's frequent visits to the

Unwinding Room to have a beer with his staff, his Greenies obviously had got the better of him. A big man, six foot in his socks, and a girth to match, Ted with his northern accent and scathing wit was a match for any Yachtsman. It was with much surprise that we got a phone call down the PO's mess from Ted, begging for some kit to be brought for'ard to hide his modesty. Ted was due to go on draft back to general service shortly, because of his belief that advancement, or lack of it, to Chief was greatly affected by Royal Yacht service. His Greenies obviously thought that it would be a good idea to de-bag him and throw him out of the mess leaving Ted with the problem of walking the Burma Road past the Warrants and Chief's mess totally naked. Lucky for us, unlucky for Ted, it was Dee the Marching Bands bass drum player who took the phone call, and proceeded for'ard with his tiger skin, this covered the front okay, but if Ted had only checked the back.

Ted's relief would turn out to be Alf, a good friend and it wouldn't be long before other Petty Officers moved aside and let other Yachtsmen move out of the Unwinding room and up the promotion ladder. All in all 1992 proved to be a good year to take over the helm from Jake; overseas commitments were few with the best being a visit to Stockholm where I had friends, and was able to fly the wife out and take a couple of days off. My boss Lt Cdr Steve Woolley was a gentleman and truly clever linguist, speaking anything from Chinese to Klingon. His faith in me from the very start was unwavering, probably because Stores was his weak subject. He was always first on my list of Officers to invite down for Sunday lunchtime; an evolution he loved apart from the mugging for his raffle money. Many a time he would say that the best atmosphere on Britannia could be found in the PO's mess, and most of the time he'd be right. The wardroom he would say was too stuffy and the Warrant and Chiefs too proper; this was probably down to the fact that our mess was the only one where everyone was the same rank. We did have infighting and power struggles, but for most, people took their jobs within the mess quite casually, with the exception of one, who I would come to call 'The Silent Assassin'.

## WINES, FINES AND FURNISHINGS

The job of Vice President of the PO's mess was never going to be an easy one especially if you were the kind of guy that never really joined in. Not being much of a drinker and certainly someone who never drank at sea he would rarely let his hair or guard down. Don't get me wrong a nice enough chap but seemed happiest when handing out fines to mess members who he considered to be breaking mess rules. One of my first tasks since joining the mess was to get the soft furnishings and carpets changed in both of the senior's messes. The carpets generally bearing the scares of the odd pint glass that had gone over in rough weather. At a time of great economic cut backs in the Navy this was going to be no easy task; using stealth, cunning and bribery I managed to get the Surveyor of Stores onboard for an inspection, and of course a couple of beers. We were completing the paperwork in the mess, and had overrun the allotted bar opening time with a beer still in hand by twelve minutes, much to the assassins great joy. As soon as the surveyor had gone, I was promptly fined a bottle of wine for every minute passed drinking up time. Conducting business for the mess in the mess, I could see was going to be a costly business, and I would be the one paying.

The new carpet arrived and was fitted, and with the new covers replacing our old very worn and stained bench seats and armchair we were ready for any set of rounds that could be thrown at us. The fine niggled at me so much, I must have worn the President down with my constant nagging, for he intervened and between the two of them they agreed to cancel my fine. All future mess deck business would be conducted in the office or up the Unwinding room, where rules were a little more relaxed, especially if the mess would benefit. I would keep a close eye on the PO's mess deck clock in future, but and even closer one on the assassin.

## TROPICAL FEVER

The biggest challenge of 1992 would haunt me to the very last day that the Yacht's company wore white tropical uniform. The stores department had issued to every Yachtsmen the previous year, two new polyester tropical outfits to replace the old cotton uniforms. This had gone well as Jake had canvassed the entire company for their sizes, instead of going off what the Navy call 'Size Rolls', these being some mathematical calculation that states if you have 200 people – you will have so many size 10, 12 , 14 and so on, it never worked.  You always had lots of the largest and smallest left over at the end of a bulk issue. Now it was to be the turn of the Officers and I had a feeling that this would not go quite so easily to plan. Our laundry crew that did such a sterling job in keeping Britain's little ambassador's looking so smart were working with very ancient steam machinery, with water straight out of a desalination plant the temperature could vary from hot to hotter. Being only able to wash at the lowest temperature of whatever the water was at that time, and press on old steam presses that would boil the water in the material itself, it became clear that the manufacturers washing instructions had been exceeded at every evolution causing shrinking of both trousers and tunics. By issuing oversized uniforms to start with we thought we might have this problem solved, only to be thwarted in every way.  It didn't matter if you ran around the upper deck every night to keep fit and the pounds off, the uniforms still didn't fit. Buttons on jackets were being strained so much, that at one point we thought someone could lose and eye should a button part company from its wearer. The Director of Music came up with his own remedy and stood fully clothed in the shower on a daily basis giving his tropical's a rinse, and the collar a scrub then just letting them drip dry in the bathroom, not something I could see the rest of the Yacht's company doing, especially the Officers, and I certainly wasn't about to suggest it to the Admiral.

## NO SHIPWRIGHTS

With more days this year than I could remember in the past being spent in Portsmouth, those that lived in or around the Portsmouth area were taking full advantage of getting home as much as possible. Even Andy the Caterer had purchased himself a property only a mile away from the dockyard gate some months earlier, and asked Derek and I to share a room. Far from being the retreat I thought it was going to be, it quickly turned into a building site, with Andy setting about lifting floorboards and sanding down everything with a nail in it. He was certainly making a good job, but I had to move back onboard very quickly; going to Andy's with the sound of a Black and Decker going off, it was just like being onboard with a dockyard matey with windy hammer banging on the deck above. If Britannia was in refit so was Andy's house. If anything the PO's mess was quieter of the two of an evening.

I had, since 1989, been very friendly with the Shipwrights, one of them John (Squiffy) living only a few miles away from me in Deal. We would travel with Mickey Joyce the Plumber and Billy, every weekend in my car sharing the expense. It was only natural that John and I would be more than just travelling companions when onboard. Together with 'Al J' the other shipwright, many an evening stuck in the dockyard would find us either in my mess or theirs (sometimes both). I'm not sure what axe the Mess President had to grind with them, but he made it his job on a daily basis to find out where the Shipwright's had spent the evening previous. If he found out that they had been my guests in the mess the night before, I would be summoned at 'Stand Easy' each forenoon for a bit of a talking to. The shout would go out 'Where's Harry the B' and when he had found me, he would repeat time and time again 'during the week when I am absent, there are to be No Shipwrights in the mess'. He knew we used to do it to wind him up; it was all good banter which was sorely missed when he did finally leave us in search of promotion. He should have stayed for the Rank of Chief; gratuity and pension would elude him.

## BUNJY JUMPING BANDIE

I have not previously changed names to protect the guilty or shield the innocent, but feel here I have to make an exception. Whilst alongside in Newcastle the whole of the Yacht was having a good time, it was after all off Royal Duty. Brewery tours had been organised, and many had taken up the offer of hospitality in the lounge afterwards, which was a lot more generous than some I had been on. In Hong Kong I remember the guide saying when we had just drank our first half, please have your other one before leaving. In Newcastle they couldn't give it away quick enough, and great restraint would have to be shown, to come out sober; most did but I believe we lost one. Getting drunk in a brewery whilst on an official tour, must have been the charge.

Having all had a good night ashore, the mess was in darkness upon our return. In the small hours of the morning the whole mess was awakened by a blood curdling scream that must have been heard as far for'ard as the Unwinding Room. As everyone piled out of their gulches into the mess square, laughter was starting to replace the shouts of' what's happening'? McD it would appear had either tried to get off the top bunk (six feet up) or had fallen out, only to find that his penis had somehow caught in the roll bar. At what height his penis and the roll bar parted company is unclear, but from the amount of blood that was now appearing around his nether regions, he might have gone the full drop. Sick Bay staff was scrambled and McD was told to get something on whilst applying pressure to his affected area. Two very loud thumps could be heard from behind his gulch curtain as McD tried to dress himself. The curtain drawn back then revealed McD in all his glory, Y fronts on back to front and football boots – hardly what you would wear to present yourself to the local hospital. His gulch mates Kegs and Derby would sort him out before he would be fit to go off for treatment. This would only leave the gulch to be cleaned up as it appeared that whilst McD was going through his penis stretching exercises, his bowels had let his down and someone with a strong stomach would be needed before sleeping could be resumed.

McD was returned to us the following morning; (looking rather 'drawn' if that's the phrase I'm looking for), wanting to show his stitches to anyone that was faintly interested for the next week, proudly stating that it took fourteen stitches to put his manhood back together. Being ordered not to get an erection for fear of causing himself more damage, mucky books started to appear on his bunk, even I had given up my latest Men Only which Kay sent me from time to time. We had all seen McD in the shower many times, and I'm sure everyone would agree – if it was fourteen stitches, it must have been micro-surgery!

## ST JAMES'S PALACE

The year went passed quicker than I had ever thought imaginable, and before I knew it we were in Leith, Scotland for a Royal Duty with almost all of the Royal family embarked. Instead of sailing south with Britannia along with three others I would drive down to attend a Divisional Petty Officers course on Whale Island. Rejoining Britannia in Portsmouth, I discovered that I had been drawn out of the hat to attend Christmas drinks with HM the Queen Mother at St James's Palace. The drinks at the Palace fell on the same day as the PO's Christmas Dance, the very event I had been helping raise money for all year. At this point I felt that I had no close friends in the mess, and as Kay didn't know any of the other wives, we would go to the Palace.

Drinks were promptly served and everyone chatted as they waited for Her Majesty to make an entrance, the doors opened and two Corgi's ambled in as if a room of strangers was normal, mine would have gone mad. The dogs made straight for Kay and sat on her feet, one on each. Her Majesty seeing this followed and ignoring everyone else in the room made straight for the wife and said 'You've got dogs haven't you' and for two minutes everyone else was ignored as they swopped dog stories.

## 1993

With the honeymoon period of a very slack programme over, it was now down to the hard work of preparing for the forthcoming deployment to the West Indies. In a 'Lay Apart Storeroom' in the dockyard, Britannia had hundreds of flags, but you could bet that the Yeoman would present me with a list of flags that we had not previously held. Awaiting receipt of these from the manufacturer before we deployed was always a harrowing time, not just for me but for the Chief Yeoman. It wasn't just a case of that flag will do, we had to have every flag in every size to suit weather conditions. If it was to be flown on one of the boats we would need a smaller breadth, and if the country had a president or Monarch we'd have a couple of those as well. All flags upon receipt would have to be checked for the correct design to ensure that a previous error was not repeated. One story goes that an unchecked USA Presidential flag was hoisted on the main mast, only to find that when it was broken open the eagle that should have been soaring skywards, had been sewn on upside down so it was plummeting to earth. As two flags were always hoisted unbroken, I understand that this was rectified almost without notice.

If I had help of any sort at these times, it was the girls in the dockyard that worked so hard on our behalf. Jackie in By Pass and Louise in local purchase were to be my saviours on many occasions, and I would have them onboard for thank you drinks very many times.

Our journey west was as always playing catch up on paperwork that had been shuffled around the trays on my desk one marked In – one Out –and one Shake it all about. At the bottom of the Shake it tray was a request for my comments on what was proposed for a future cut to Royal Yacht crew numbers. A ten percent reduction of crew would, we were told, ensure the Yacht's future, making her more streamlined financially. It was proposed that Naval Stores staff could be reduced by one, as we only had three Killicks, I quickly worked it out that my staff was to go down by thirty three percent. I'm sure that DSO noted my comments but didn't want to repeat them.

Normally three weeks after sailing would find our paperwork up to date, storerooms gleaming and ready for rounds, it would seem that should we take the manpower cut, it would be not just all hands to the pumps, but pump harder there aren't so many of you. A quick call into May port would find the great number of the Warrant and Chief's mess returning to the Yacht, dressed in full No1 uniform just before leave expired, having evidently all just had breakfast in McDonalds; why and whose idea I never found out, but they certainly looked the business. Our Guard Ship a frigate joined us, and it was straight into Royal Duty. An invite for twenty Senior

Yachtsmen to be accompanied by twenty seniors from our Guard Ship was received onboard to attend a Bar B Q in Little Cayman. Having got drawn out of the hat yet again, it was straight into civvies shirt and tie, with our counterparts wearing their best, whatever that was. Britannia used her boats for liberty men and we picked up our general service counterparts on the way. No need for introductions as it was a very low key affair, but one of the chaps from the frigate stormed in and started offering his hand to anyone who looked like they might shake it, saying very loudly 'Hello I'm petty Officer Smyth, Royal Navy' – not to be out done and with a quieter voice I said 'Harry The B – Royal Yacht' It was game set and match. Calls followed in Kingston and Martinique before Royal Duty ended and those that had wives flying out could prepare to wind down, for those that hadn't, hopefully there would be many chances of lots of time off.

## WOWTR'S AIRWAYS

With the WOWTR once more running his travel club, the ladies were scheduled to arrive in St Lucia the day before Britannia berthed, giving them a chance to recover from jet lag. Being stuck in Martinique and St Lucia being only a forty dollar flight away was more than we could bear, so the plan to island hop by plane was hatched. By jumping on a plane we could land at the north airstrip of the island and be in the hotel two hours before the girls landed at the south airstrip. The plan worked well apart from the fact Rob had told no one he was scared of flying on small planes. Had any of us seen this before hand, we would have all had reservations. The plane didn't exactly stop, more slowed to a crawl, as we all threw our baggage onboard and followed as quickly as possible. With the door to the cockpit still flapping and the back door in the process of being shut we took off. We arrived safely only to have all the flowers we had purchased for the wives being confiscated by customs. The girls arrived in St Lucia and having a two hour mini bus ride up to us from the South would have gone through Castries the capital. Seeing no Royal Yacht in the harbour I guess they would have thought it was party time. When Kay disembarked from her taxi, I came up behind her and said in a deep voice, 'carry your bags lady' she couldn't believe it, we all truly delivered a surprise for all the girls!

It's a long way to go for the ladies, but it was bliss. Happy hour had to be attended on pain of death. It was a Royal Yacht reunion both lunchtime and evening, we even ended up hiring the barman 'Felix' when he said he had a mini bus, and ended up with a full island tour including lunch for about twenty dollars.

Playing volleyball one lunchtime I kicked the ball in bare feet and paid the price by pushing my big toe backwards, very silly and very painful. Luckily Eric the Doc was on hand and prescribing lots of ice cold foot baths, the swelling went down, but not enough for the foot to be used for walking. Eric a very big chap compared to myself, ended up carrying me on his back everywhere to ensure I wouldn't either miss it or be late – cheers, one I owe you.

Taking time out of the hotel and finding a restaurant overlooking the harbour, we came across John, Don, Al J and Chubby the Can Man from the Chief's mess eating team, and were promptly asked to join them. All was in full flow when Chubby excused himself to go to the little boy's room, only to miss his dinner being served at the table by a minute. Not wanting his food to go cold, we started to set about the French fries, before eyeing up his steak. After about ten minutes Chubby had still not returned, when we despatched a search party, well Squiffy to look for him. Chubby was found slumped in the toilets having suffered, what we thought could be a mild heart attack. With this firmly established his steak was divided and devoured, much to Kay's amazement. We explained that he wouldn't have wanted it now anyway. Chubby would be flown to Martinique where the French hospital facilities were more advanced. We wondered if he would be going on the aircraft we had come in on; he would have a heart attack! Chubby returned to us a few days later, but would be watching his diet for a long time after that. Once the girls had returned to UK, our business continued taking in another ten ports of call with the Duke of Edinburgh.

To provide entertainment a Sods Opera had been planned, and in Britannia style in would be a grand affair. On a warship these things are thrown together almost overnight, but of course with The Duke sat in the front row, acts would have to be rehearsed, polished and presented to the committee to make sure they are not only suitable, but most of all acceptable; bad language and nudity completely banned thankfully. As always the PO's mess act would be arranged by the PTI who had decided to put on a boxing match, he was spoilt for choice as half the mess wanted to take part. In the end Frenchy the chef (the biggest chap in the mess) and I (almost the smallest) were pitted together as the boxers, and mayhem ruled. The Warrant and Chiefs stole the show with their synchronised dit, and even the Household did a sketch; a night for the Duke to remember I'm sure. All the acts with the exception of Simon Dungy's went down well, for you couldn't hear from his 'Blakey' from on the buses impression for shouts of 'Ere –Ere' from the audience, Simon's trademark call. You'd have thought he was Cornish, but this was a Southampton accent everyone took the rise out of unmercifully.

Royal Duty ended in Palm Beach with Prince Edward joining us for the final Sea Day. It had been a hectic schedule, not including the break in St Lucia and we soon were heading our way across the pond, looking forward to some Easter leave. We would have one month in Portsmouth, long enough to restore and complete maintenance which, like storing, was an ongoing evolution. Our next five months were to be in UK waters, with calls in London, Sunderland, Hartlepool, and Hull and of course Cowes and Western

Isles. It was going to be like Island hopping around the West Indies without the sun shine.

## THE BATTLE OF HASTINGS

After dinner entertainment for Her Majesty during the Western Isles cruise was normally taken care of by the band, but every now and again the Senior Engineer, whose job it was for some reason to arrange this, would try and put on something different. Having proved myself during our fund raising for the Band Disaster Fund concert, I was asked if I can perform a Stanley Holloway monologue in front of the Royals. Reluctantly due to nerves I agreed, believing that it wouldn't do my standing as a Yachtsman any harm. I decided to go all out and involved both Shipwrights and the painter Martin to making me up some props. Wooden sword and shield and brown paper sack turned into a tunic, complete with Red Cross and coat of arms. The result when worn with sea boot stockings, black fire fighting boots, anti flash hood and gloves looked ridiculous. If the monologue didn't get a laugh then surely my outfit would. Having practised my lines over and over again, it was show time. Being introduced to the assembled Royals as Harry The B by the Director of Music, I marched straight in and stood opposite Her Majesty as close to the table as I dare, before starting the monologue. Seventeen verses all rhyming in a very bad northern accent, and no room for error in front of half the Royal Family. Mission accomplished, with my knees knocking and my breath coming in short gasps I bowed turned around and walked out. I could hear the Duke of Edinburgh in full voice repeating the last line before breaking into laughter,' *ON HIS HORSE, WITH HIS HAWK, IN HIS HAND*'. A quick thank you from the keeper and steward of the household, and that's your lot. No photographs allowed but luckily Paul Bateman had caught sight of me and produced a drawing, the man has talent.

Together with Nick Nicholson from our TYS show, we would go down and entertain on several occasions, and if I told the story of the Battle of Trafalgar; he would do all the actions. If he was doing his magic act I would dress up as his assistant, with false boobs and a beard how convincing. We would normally get Harry the Back to just sweep up in the back ground with a cigarette hanging out of his mouth, this always brought the house down for some reason.

## BED PAN PLEASE NURSE

We sailed for India in the September, and with plenty of time managed a quick brake with wives in Malta, before hosting the Central Heads of Government meeting in Limassol, and Sea Days in Bosphorous and Piraeus. Having disembarked the Royal in Cyprus, the decision to hang around the area was made on a medical basis. Andy and Eric were having a nightmare in the Sickbay, we seemed to have got a severe case of the trots onboard, with Yachtsmen falling like flies, and being unable to leave the heads for more than a few minutes at a time. It was clear we had a problem, just how big a problem the PMO had yet to find out. With over forty of the Yacht's company confined to their bunks, and queues outside the heads, an RAF food poisoning investigation team was despatched to us, in the hope of getting to the bottom of it, no pun intended. A ward was established ashore in the air base at Akrotiri, where the most serious of our walking wounded were placed on drips, being after all this time, dehydrated. It must have been sheer hell for the sick, but for the likes of so many others who didn't go down with it, it was a bar b q every afternoon on the beach. I would visit the hospital of an evening and make sure everyone had batteries for their walkmans and anything else that had been requested to take ashore. If I heard the shout 'Nurse Bed Pan quickly' (once I heard it a dozen times), they were going through hell, my right hand man Spud being one of them. Finally getting over the bug, a cocktail party for all Yachtsmen was held on the Royal deck, the only place big enough to say thank you to the staff of the hospital, from all the crew. A Yacht's plaque was duly presented, to be placed on the door of the newly named 'Britannia Ward'. The cause of the food poisoning was put down to a batch of eggs we had brought with us from the UK. They had made an appearance on the menu twice on the day in question, once in the Scotch eggs and again in the salad, both it would appear to be popular choices – Not with me ,Unlucky Chaps.

With four days taken out of the programme, we would have a bit of a race on our hands to get to Dammam to rendezvous with Prince Charles, but with Britannia at full speed, we would get there just in time.

## MIDDLE EAST AND INDIA

In Abu Dhabi we were to host the British Trade week, which meant that the chance of a run ashore would be limited. Our hosts must have foreseen this for the Jetty was lined with food tents, and free telephone boxes courtesy of the Sheik Khalifa. For those that had suffered in Cyprus it was a chance to put some weight back on, so it was steak morning noon and night. Ian the Caterer must have been laughing as he watched his account go into credit, having all but shut the galleys down onboard. Leaving the Middle East behind it was off to Bombay, where we would host commercial receptions onboard of a daily basis. We would enter and leave harbour every day, which meant the dress ship flags, would be hoisted in the morning at morning colours, lowered on leaving harbour, hoisted when we returned and lowered again at sunset. As we would normally be on deck for an hour, upon entering or leaving harbour, we were all to get a lovely sun tan on two lower arms, two lower legs and a face. Again a run ashore was restricted by time to a couple of hours in the afternoon; just as well the bazaar was only up the road as Bombay was not the place to be spending an evening walking the streets. The Sea Days were a complete success with Britannia showing off the best of British and doing it in style.

## VICTUALLED MEMBERS ONLY

One of the great occasions in Portsmouth harbour if time allowed, was a gathering of the victualled members of both Senior Yachtsmen's messes. At this time thirteen of us were living onboard, going home only at weekends if you were not part of the Duty Watch, and of course main leave periods. Once a year if we could recruit Eric the Admiral's steward, Badger to wash up and most importantly the Officer of The Day to donate a bottle of port, a successful evening could be guaranteed. When all the Warrants and Chiefs that lived ashore had gone home for the evening, we would set about transforming the mess; tables that barely fitted through hatches had to come up from the dining halls, all overseen by Squiffy at the top, Al J at the bottom, a clockwork operation unless Gobbler the Chief Yeoman got involved. This of course had to be reversed at the end of an evening, which always took longer for some reason.

## NEW YORK 1994

It was cold enough in the UK when we sailed for the USA, and weather reports for the eastern seaboard weren't that clever. A fuel stop in Bermuda before tackling the Hudson River, which at this time still had free flowing ice, enough of the stuff in fact to cause concern to the Engineers, should it block up our intakes and stop us making fresh water. We also could not ignore the fact that the river might freeze delaying us for the next part of our programme in warmer climes. With the Big Apple being a big bad city, we were all advised to go ashore in pairs. Richard the Canteen Assistant obviously ignored the warning and walked ashore on his own, only to be pulled over by New York's finest late in the evening 'You gotta be careful out there – this place is dangerous' he was told – 'I know I've nearly slipped over twice' he replied in his thick northern tongue pointing to some ice on the sidewalk. This leaving two very bemused Policeman scratching their heads.

From New York to Belize where we were joined by Her Majesty, and Britannia steamed her one-millionth mile (that's equal to the moon and back twice); this did not go without undue celebration onboard, and certificates were given to the whole Yacht's company. Once home we were to prepare for D Day remembrance, this was to be the biggest review ever. Liberty ships were coming over from America, and Heads of State from all over the world would be onboard. With the Yacht's company at Man Ship stations, we would witness the embarkation of some of the world's most powerful people. When President Clinton stepped onto the Jetty from his motorcade, he just looked at Britannia with awe. He must have thought 'Air Force One' paled in comparison to the splendour that was now before him. It wasn't the brightest of days but with the crew lining the side, all flags flying and the band playing, Britannia must have looked a picture.

## ROYAL GARDEN PARTY

To commemorate the Forty years of Britannia, all Yachtsmen past and present, were invited to attend a garden party at Buckingham Palace. As I was born the same year the Yacht was launched, it was perhaps fitting that the party fell just the day after my birthday. Walking around the grounds dressed in Uniform with Kay on my arm, it was an amazing afternoon. The normal bun fight to get anywhere near the Royal Party ensued, so we just stayed in the back ground, and enjoyed the day for what it was – magic.

## ST PETERSBURG

For two months I had been searching every Naval Establishment and Supply base trying to locate two hundred and fifty ceremonial greatcoats, one each for the Yacht's company. It was planned for Her Majesty to visit Russia, the first by any British Monarch since the revolution. The plan was for the Yacht's company to line the route from Britannia to the Cenotaph in St Petersburg. Our journey to Russia would involve a stopover in Aberdeen for fuel, and the best of all marching practise. At this time I had been onboard for nine years and had only marched for one hour, whilst in HMS Raleigh on PO's course. To say the Yacht's company were out of practise would not be putting too finer point on it. The greatcoats supplied were in two sizes, large and very large and so had to be issued on a 'that nearly fits you basis'. We didn't have to wear them in Aberdeen, which is just as well with the local fishermen looking on; they may have lost any faith they had in the Royal Navy.

Assembled on the Jetty the Sgt Royal Marines was to put us through our paces. It was bad enough just being sized and put into marching squads, but when the order quick march was given, all hell broke loose. Some started on the left foot, some on the right but most noticeable of all was we were all going at a different pace. With one squad catching another and one falling back, it was obvious that the Sgt had his work cut out. Things did start to improve with a bit of practise, up to the point when Daisy the Charge Chief lost a shoe, and rather than scramble around for it, marched on regardless. The result being everyone behind him tripping up over his lost property, and laughing in the process at this rather large man limping at the head of the column. Trying to regain control the shout of 'Halt for Christ sake' from the Sgt was mostly unheard due to the laughter. We were a shambles, of that there is no denying, but we were a happy shambles and given a few more laps of the jetty were finally getting the hang of it. It would transpire that we would not be required for this event, and in the end only four people would attend the Cenotaph ceremony. The Sgt must have breathed the biggest sigh of relief in his life.

Our only other mishap in Russia came in the shape of a sleek grey messenger of death called HMS Glasgow. We had been together in the past when she had been our guard ship, and had got on very well with her ships company. Receiving an invitation to drinks onboard at the lunchtime, was just poor timing – for the party spilled back to our mess in Britannia, and before we knew it Her Majesty was due to embark.

Making sure Billy got off his bunk, dressed as he was in Blue Suit and medals, was down to his own department, and to their credit had him ready to go in no time. There were some merry Petty Officers on Man Ship that day, but luckily the jetty was a good hundred yards away and although the press were out in force, they weren't really looking at us. Our saving grace is that with all the marching practise in Aberdeen, we had all gone on, and off in step and on time, and the matter was never mentioned again.

The ten percent reduction in crew went ahead, with Spud doing the decent thing, and putting himself ahead of Andy and Geoff. He volunteered to go back to general service. Spud would be due his PO's rate soon, and knew that he would have had to have left Britannia anyway. It was a good call, although I would miss his banter; what I wouldn't miss was his red eyes and the way he would hold his head in one hand, whilst shuffling the same piece of paper around the desk all morning, after a good run ashore, off Royal Duty of course. Not even a plea from Andy to accompany him to the storeroom to hide would make him leave his desk.

## OUT OF THE HAT 'AGAIN'

Returning to home port would see us anchor overnight at Spithead, due to severe gale force winds which would prevent us from berthing, so some mess games would pass the evening. Smurf suggested we revive the old 'Koala' championships, and stripped off to demonstrate. Now dressed only in his underwear he climbed a square pole situated at the end of the bar, and using both hands and feet hung on for as long as possible. Paul Beal came next and produced a very respectable time, it was obviously a small man's game, as both Paul and Smurf were built like whippets. I gave it my best, but lacked in every department and was soon handing over to a very keen PTI. Whilst Andy was stripping off in his gulch, we were busying ourselves polishing the pole with everything we could find. We got some serious amounts of polish on the pole before Andy made his assent, only to find he was on his backside quicker than that, the look on his face was priceless. Smurf was declared the outright winner, retaining his title.

Once in Port I couldn't believe my luck. For years I had not been selected to take my wife to any Royal functions, when last year I had been drawn for the Queen Mothers drinks, this year I had come out of the hat for the Buckingham Palace Christmas ball. I could feel everybody's eyes on me when my name was called out. I wasn't exactly popular, but after years in the Invite wilderness I wasn't about to move aside. Daisy booked the 'Reuben's Hotel' in Buckingham Palace Road, which meant not only could we meet up for an aperitif before descending on the Palace, but there would be no scramble for a taxi afterwards. Having been fully briefed by Rear Admiral Woodard about where to be in the Palace and at what time, we assembled to await the arrival of the Royal Family. FORY had obviously studied military tactics, for this was the perfect place to spring his trap. The passageway the Royals used narrowed at this point, so as the Royal party made their way past we were introduced to all of the Royals present. It was Daisy again that suggested we steer away from black tie and wear something a little different. I opted for the matching 'Dennis the Menace tie and cummerbund set' whilst Daisy went for the Interflora look. The comments from the Prince of Wales being 'like the ties chaps'. It was a night that Kay and I will remember for the rest of our lives.

## CAPE TOWN AND COMMODORE'S 1995

With the ten percent reduction in crew starting to bite, it would appear even those at the top were not to be spared the defence cuts. Rear Admiral Woodard (FORY) would be replaced on our visit to South Africa by Commodore Morrow. With no other ship in the Royal Navy having a Commodore in command, flags in all sizes would have to be specially made just for the Royal Yacht, along with all the headed stationery being reprinted and of course all publicity leaflets. Demands had been placed as soon as this announcement was made, and on the morning of sailing everything for the new Commodore turned up; that was cutting it fine even for me.
We sailed in early January and after the customary rounds and getting all the office work up to speed, I was now the office junior as well as the office senior, so I would clean the scuttle and start to look for that Squeegee I'd offered the chef on Endurance!. We called into Abidjan and Walvis Bay for fuel and a reception, before quietly slipping into Simons Town without arousing the local media. The purpose of this deception was to await the arrival of Her Majesty who as always would fly out, but here we needed it to look as if Her Majesty had sailed with us as we went into Cape Town.

When we came out of the mist into the harbour in Cape Town, thousands lined the jetty and the harbour entrance.

Nelson Mandela was waiting on the jetty as we slid into our berth, the atmosphere being electric. South Africa isolated from the Commonwealth for so many years, was making a comeback. If there was ever a more enthusiastic welcome for Britannia, I can't think where it was. We would visit Durban for a brief visit before making our way back to Cape Town again; and this time it would be Kay and the other wives on the jetty. WOWTR had put his travel agents hat on again. The wives had the opportunity to travel round to Simons Town onboard, which was a real treat for them all. Finding Eddie Yates in the wheelhouse was a bonus, as he handed over the wheel to Kay and for five minutes, with the Officer of the Watches permission steered a steady course around the Cape not a bad claim to fame. Once in Port we discovered there was no transport to take us back to our hotel in Cape Town and with only a couple of cabs available, it was everyman for themselves. Kay and I squeezed in with the BBC team, but others had to wait for the cabs doing a round trip which took them ages.

 One bright morning we decided to take a kaffa cab (not used during apartheid) out to a beach, only to find the cab running us back through a township made out of forty five gallon oil drums before depositing us in a place called Weinberg. He would only take us back to Cape Town for forty dollars, a sum of money I didn't have and if I did wasn't going to part with. Seeing we were the only white people in the town centre we hastily made our way up the street, in the hope of finding a proper taxi, only to stumble upon a young girl just about to pull the driveway gates closed. On the gatepost the sign said 'Armed response – all Intruders will be Shot' this was the place for us. Introducing ourselves the owner Dr Jeremy Royds and his wife Trish ushered inside and sat us down by the swimming pool, where a bar b q was in full swing. We couldn't believe our luck, one minute we are in fear of having our throats cut, the next we are being treated like royalty ourselves. The least I could do was to invite them onboard to say thank you, without Kay unfortunately who would have flown home by this time.

The BBC had also put in an appearance making a documentary about Britannia, and as many Yachtsmen as possible were being encouraged to talk openly about their time onboard. I expect I will go down in history for revealing how many toilet rolls we would get through on a monthly basis, or how much washing up liquid the galley would use over a six month period. Although the programme would not make me a star, at home those that didn't know I was on Britannia – did now! My cover had been blown.

## END OF AN ERA

Our period of station leave was only granted to those that could be spared; those required daily had to report in, and everybody had to be onboard the day Rear Admiral Robert Woodard was to leave. With many rounds of goodbyes already said, the final day came and FORY'S horse and carriage were waiting on the Jetty. One by one he shook hands with every member of the Yacht's company, thanking them for their hard work and loyalty. It didn't surprise me that when he wished me well he knew my wife's name; he'd met her almost as many times as he had met me. as I'd flown her out so much. Like a scene from the film 'In which we Serve' he addressed all two hundred Yachtsmen by their Christian names without the aid of a prompt or photo board. During his five years in command he had fully involved himself with the workings of the Yacht at the lower level, and always said that that was where the real people lived. To the tune of 'Black Adder' a tune he hated, and one that the band played at his dinner parties to let him know they had done enough; he was taken down the brow to his awaiting carriage.

Not everyone agreed with the Admirals style of command, having a drink with the lads on many occasions and keeping up with gossip on the lower deck. I had accepted a couple of invites in the past to his cabin for a drink and a chat, only excusing myself when time was getting late. It was well known that FORY could talk well into the small hours. I had seen grown men run away from the PO's bar when he was looking for an ear or two to attend his cabin. I will remember him for the day he escorted Prince Charles into the mess, and asked me to entertain him, which along with Smurf and Mick Currell I tried but; Mick had served as a stoker on a ship with the Prince, and relayed the story of when the Prince had patted his stomach and warned him he was putting on weight. Mick was even bigger now in the stomach department and with his stammer said to the Prince 'Yoo o o uu we were rr right Ssir' as he patted his beer belly.

Our journey home would follow the same route as of our passage south, arriving in the UK at the beginning of May. Our programme for the rest of the year had been firmed up, and it was clear that we were in for some very busy periods of Royal Duty. We would visit four UK ports in quick succession and visits to Rendsburg and Kiel, before being able to settle down into our normal routine. Cowes and Western Isles, and yet another trip to the Pool of London, which was fast beginning to feel like Royal Yacht Moorings in Whale Island but with better scenery. VJ celebration fireworks lighting up Britannia and Tower Bridge, only this time I wasn't given a camera to record it. The talk on the lower deck at this time was when and how the Yacht would make her final exit from the public eye. With Officers turning over appointments onboard every couple of years, I had yet another new boss, and had been asked to prepare a de-store plan for the entire contents of Britannia, including manpower and time scales. Only ever having completed this task in theory at the Supply School, it was clear Andy, Geoff and I would be in for a very busy period, when this did finally happen.

## BUSINESS AS USUAL 1996

If Britannia were to be saved, we could have done with two things Good Publicity and even more Good Publicity. We didn't get either. Even our prime time documentary on BBC with Swampy saying 'Britannia looks like a graceful swan on the water, what you don't see is us lot paddling like mad underneath' failed to win us any votes. We were doomed, of that we were sure, we just didn't know when. Most were fairly certain it wouldn't or couldn't happen this year as the programme was out, and although it didn't look too outrageous, it was pretty much all go until September. Once more we would be heading west for Royal Duty again in Palm Beach.

## THE MG AFFAIR

It wouldn't be the run ashore that would prove to be a problem in Palm Beach, but the coming back. I had gone ashore with Steve the PO steward, so was guaranteed to return only having had a couple of beers. Steve and I returned quite late to find the mess in darkness and in the corner quietly sobbing was someone I shall call MG. Trying to find out what the problem was, proved difficult but both of us heard him say something about shooting a taxi driver, or a taxi driver being shot. Realizing this was well out of our pay band and a potential hand grenade, we decided that the Officer of the Day should be informed. It was my misfortune that this Officer happened to be my Boss; relaying what I had been told by MG in the mess he was all ears. Unbeknown to me MG was now in the Sick Bay inventing a whole new story, and no amount of explaining on my part would convince Lt Cdr Tulley that what I had told him was the truth. I had witnesses but he wouldn't listen, accusing me of being able to embellish a good story. The boss's 'Invites' to the mess on a Sunday stopped; perhaps I should have got **MG** to invite him.

Savannah would follow and an invite ashore by the Mayor for as many Yachtsmen that could be spared duty. Over a hundred of us crowded into one room, where sat in the middle was the bench from the film 'Forrest Gump' and each in turn having the obligatory photo whilst saying 'Life is like a box of Chocolates'. Band Sgt Johnson was the most convincing, but his nickname was Forrest behind his back anyway, so he should have done.

## BALTIMORE BOAT RACE

If the USA has any claim to fame where old ships are concerned, then it would be the USS Constitution, known as Old Ironsides. Still sitting in the water, with her bilge pumps constantly running flat out, fighting what appears to be on the outside a losing battle against decay and water ingress. She is advertised as the oldest ship afloat, and may be, but HMS Victory can give her a few years, and although her bottom is in a dry dock, she is still the oldest ship in the RN in Commission, Britannia at this time being of course the second! Accepting an invitation from the Baltimore and Hull lifesaving museums to have a rowing race in an Admirals 'Skiff' was an opportunity not to be missed, and as our team would have had no experience in these craft they would even give us a bit of coaching. Getting a crew from Britannia together was easy and no shortage of volunteers, but the hard part would be pulling these huge craft. On our first outing the lads must have put in such an effort it rattled the museums into thinking, here is a race they could lose. Our crew were not so sure, one thing to row across the harbour, another to do it for a mile and a half. With tactics being drawn up onboard, the crew decided to dress in one of the Yacht's rugby strips, if they couldn't be winners they would certainly be the best dressed losers. On a cold morning Britannia's finest (well those that volunteered) prepared to do battle for the honour of the Yacht. It was probably my steering, or the fact I lost my voice and couldn't call the stroke, but 'Woody' on stroke oar kept everyone together. We came in a very respectable four boat lengths behind. The beer would be on us in the Unwinding Room, 'where the truth would out'. They had got rattled when they saw that our team could pull, so not only did they pull in all their best rowers, and they had lots to choose from, they also stitched us up into carrying a passenger.

## EASTERN SEABOARD 1996

With our defeat well and truly behind us, it was on to Boston, for a mixture of Royal and Commercial Duty, before we could relax and head off to Toronto. We had had four Diplomatic and Commercial reception and seminars in four days. Getting as much out of Britannia as was possible before she was laid up, was mentioned many times. Once in Toronto and with a changed schedule it appeared that I might be able to get some family onboard from a place called 'Drumbo' in the tobacco country about an hour away, and also might be able to disappear for a couple of days as well. Getting names from the family of those who wanted to visit, I was astounded when twenty four of the family had all come forward. I would need help, as the rules state only four guests per Yachtsmen at any one time. With the promise of a couple of days at home in Drumbo, I set about finding volunteers to help me out. Dave, Ginge, Alf and Bozzie came to my rescue, which meant the Canadian side of the family had a good tour, and we all got the weekend off. Nice one chaps!

# SLIX

With just the crossing of the pond in front of us, we would stop for fuel in Halifax. It was during the fuelling that I was approached by the engineers for some oil dispersant or 'Slix' as it was known; something they normally held by the drum load for the occasional oil spill. Finding none onboard, and not having any funds at the end of the financial year to pay for it, I said I would approach the company that were pumping hundreds of pounds worth of diesel oil into us. The manager Adrian was summoned and with a quick tour round, he promised to help. It turned out Adrian was in a bit of a quandary, he had invites onboard for himself and his wife that night to a Wardroom reception, but his secretary was feeling left out and was desperate to get onboard. Going to see Topsy the Chief Electrician who had taken over as Cox'n, he agreed that I could, even at this late stage, get Adrian and his secretary on the guest list for that afternoon.

No sooner had we finished fuelling when the Slix arrived, and the gangway opened for guests, Adrian was waiting. With the tour done it was down to the mess for a beer, before Adrian had to disappear with the secretary, get changed and return with his wife for the official reception. Minus travelling time, he must have spent more time on board that day than I did.

Our journey home was uneventful apart from when we passed over the spot where Titanic had sunk; upper deck viewing space was at a premium, with most of the Yacht's company reflecting on what happened here in this desolate ocean so many years before.

With the Chiefs of Staff meeting to be hosted onboard two days after we arrived, there were no prizes for guessing what the subject up for discussion would be, although we were taking bets on the timings. Commodore Morrow would clear lower deck and let us know the latest score on the Yacht's fate, it would take miracles rather than money to save Britannia.

## THE RUBBISH SKIP

With a trip over the Irish Sea and duty in both Belfast and Londonderry, we made our way back stopping in the Isle of Man. Never having been to Douglas along with several others I went ashore, before Prince Charles joined us the following day. Being at anchor meant liberty boat routine and this could always be a bit more hit and miss as far as returning is concerned. The boats don't wait, if you're not on the jetty come the last liberty boat, that's your own fault. For Eddie Yates and Mick Gentry this was to be the case, missing that last boat meant they would have to fend for themselves until the first boat back in the morning. The jetty at Douglas offered very little in the way of shelter from the weather, so it must have come as a relief to find not just a skip, but a clean skip. Eddie and Mick were the kind of chaps that you wouldn't want to be behind in the queue for the ironing board, both fastidious over their appearance. I would have given a day's pay, not to see them climb in the skip the night before, but to watch them emerge the following morning. Both dressed in Suits, razor sharp creases in their trousers, without as much as a speck of dirt on them. They bragged not only had the skip been cleaned, it had been lined with fresh cardboard, luxury. I still reckon they must have slept standing up.

## THE QUEEN MOTHER'S WALKROUND

Her Royal Highness embarked at Marchwood for a reception to be held in Falmouth. There was lots of speculation that she wouldn't use Britannia anymore because of the lack of a lift, and with the geography of the Yacht, a trip or a fall could be waiting around any corner. When news of the walk round hit the messes it was clear that it would be standing room only. Being introduced, I recalled to her the story of her corgi's sitting on my wife's feet at the Christmas drinks party in 1992. She didn't remember my wife but remembered the incident, and said that the corgis always broke the ice at receptions, to the point of trying to upstage her. Not a hand went unshaken or a person unspoken to, as she made her way around the mess. 1996 would not eventually go down as being our busiest, with just Royal and Diplomatic receptions in Amsterdam, before our final visit to Cowes and our penultimate Western Isles cruise. The rest of our year would be spent in Portsmouth, with essential works being carried out to ensure that out final year would go without any hitches. A closed drafting routine had been put in force; anybody who was still on Britannia now, would serve until the end. Promotions would be made, if you could be accommodated in the mess to which you will be promoted. Yachtsmen took the advantage of the time to sort themselves out with courses in preparation of their returning to general service, a prospect which not one long standing Yachtsmen looked forward to.

## THE FINAL YEAR 1997

This was it then, the programme was set and a very busy six months lay ahead. Sailing from Portsmouth on the 20th January, Port visits were to come around at a very fast rate. High commission reception in Malta, Royal and Commercial visits in the Middle East with Britannia standing up to the pace giving a good account of herself. After a four month period in Portsmouth she looked as grand as she had ever done. No one could have predicted what was to come next.

# THE COMING TOGETHER

Taking fuel from a moving tanker at sea whilst under way, is
something Britannia has done more times than I've had runs ashore
(and I've had a few). Well practised drills from the sailors on the
upper deck, combined with the expertise of the stokers down below,
ensured that the practise of bringing two ships together went without
incident. Steaming along side by side at about ten knots, would mean
that the helmsman would have to steer into the tanker, to avoid being
pushed aside by its wake.

 There is a law that states if something is going to break, it will break
at the worst possible moment – and for us this was it. With no answer
from the helm, Britannia quickly crossed over the point of no return,
and a 25,000 ton tanker was going to eat a 4,500 ton Royal Yacht for
breakfast. The Royal Marine band playing on the bridge wing, along
with the guy on the distance line, would have been the first to see the
Auxiliary ship Bayleaf getting just that bit too close for comfort.
Those down below didn't know anything about it until we actually
met. With the Band running to the port bridge wing and all sirens
blasting – we arrived. The damage could have been so much worse,
and the fact we lost no lives must certainly not be overlooked. A
stoker in the stabiliser compartment was to be the luckiest of all,
having just moved from behind the stabiliser housing to see it all
being pushed in behind him. With Bayleaf scraping down the whole
length of Britannia, guardrails, gunwales and decking started to
buckle under the weight of the collision. Lengths of guardrails with
their brass edges started to drop onto Bayleaf's decks and were being
brandished as trophies. Once apart, damage to both vessels could be
assessed, and without a doubt it looked like the Bayleaf had the
better of us.

The Bayleaf's side showed nothing more than a few deep scars, with a bit of Royal Blue and Gold leaf for colouring. We on the other hand looked like a bar piano keyboard, bit dented, bit scratched and bits missing, but still seaworthy. The thing that must have suffered the most is the Commodore's pride, there would be lots of questioned asked onboard and in the Admiralty.

Having got a good idea of what we needed to put Britannia right and with maintenance period in Sembawang dockyard already scheduled in, it was decided to continue with our programme. The only consideration being that we would berth alongside always 'port side to', this giving those prying eyes of the public and press very little to look at, unless they wanted to hire a boat and go around to the disengaged side. Even then with the emergency screens covering most of the damage, there wasn't a lot to see.

Our commercial Sea Days in Pakistan and India went without any hitches, and between ports our general routine of cleaning and preparing for the next Royal Duty went unchanged. John the Chippy could often be seen on both hands and knees, pulling out any old caulking from between the teak deck planks that had blown, and would allow water to settle underneath. With eight laps of the upper deck being almost a mile in length, there must have been over a hundred miles of caulking to keep an eye on. On many an occasion I would approach John whilst in the middle of his labours, and knowing that I was going to give him a bit of ribbing, he would always say before I could get a word out 'and you can @$!& off'.

## NAUSHIRWAN P. DUBASH

Attending a reception at the High Commission is something that Petty Officers are not normally invited to do, but on this occasion the presence of four senior Yachtsmen had been requested. The last thing I was expecting was to be introduced to someone that used to holiday in Broadstairs on the Isle of Thanet. We had in common a family of Café owners the 'Morellis', he being a personal friend, and I having worked for them as a teenager. We got on immediately and before leaving he invited all four Senior Yachtsmen back for a private function he was having at his house three days later. Already having invited his family onboard as our guests, we accepted and thought no more about it.

Having our invite to the Dubash family residence cancelled by the Visit Liaison Officer, came as a bit of a shock to all parties concerned. We understood that the private function he was to hold had been seen as a Wardroom invite, and one that should not be shared. Consulting WOWTR for advise, something I had frequently done since being rated PO, he went ballistic saying 'that's not on – I'll sort it'. Being then called to the Liaison Officer's cabin only to be told that the four Senior's can now attend the function, was like waving the red flag at a bull. Calling a meeting of Steve Barlow, Andy the PTI, Ginge and myself, we decided the only way forward was to not only attend the function, we would go in the Officer's transport.

Naushirwan greeted Officers and seniors warmly, showing the Officer's to a table at the back and us to a table with his daughter's at the front. An unforgettable evening followed, and although the laughter was mostly from our table it was from his family. Transport booked to return at 2300 hrs, but we had instructions to stay behind, and as soon as we were there alone the party started in earnest. Nothing was too much trouble from a phone call home each, to a lift back to Britannia in his convertible Cadillac, with son Danesh at the wheel. The Dubash family made it onboard as our guests the following day, being greeted at the top of the brow by the Liaison Officer with nothing more than a frown, and a salute.

## PHUKET

Phuket had been on the programme from day one, and was a chance of two days R & R to each watch. Even I had been given a couple of days, which surprised me as I was bringing Kay out later in the trip. Ashore the first evening with Steve Green, we came across a young English girl very much the worse for wear. Sobering her up and getting her back to her vessel the 'Mylin IV' was to be our good deed of the day, and resulted in a visit from their Captain. The Mylin being a dry vessel (no alcohol) he showed his appreciation ashore with a couple of beers and a T shirt each. We never did find out who the owner was, the whole ship was cloaked in secrecy, and the crew had done the owner proud, for not one of them would reveal his or her identity, even after a few beers.

## THE RICKSHAW RACE

Having moved round to Penang for an informal visit, I received an invite from the Warrant and CPO's eating team to join them ashore for a meal, and I took it. I don't think the plan was to go by Trishaw but seeing them all lined up on the jetty, the temptation was too much. Getting into pairs and selecting our steeds the bet was on, five dollars to the driver who could reach the restaurant first. The pace to start whilst we were on the flat was quite reasonable, but with a hill fast approaching things were to slow down rapidly. A larger financial investment would have to be made to secure first place.
Three out of the four Trishaws were to arrive at the restaurant in a reasonable time, but what had happened to Don Smith and the Chubby the Can Man? It was another heart attack, not Chubby this time, but the Trishaw driver. They obviously picked the driver with a forty a day habit or they were driving him too hard on the last hill.

Chubby and Don missed the meal, but earned a pint or two providing the laughter.

## PASSPORT PROBLEMS

As this was to be Britannia's and mine last deployment, I had let Rob talk me into the trip of a lifetime for our ladies. They were to fly out and join us in Kuala Lumpur, and we would follow Britannia down south by train. All four of us finding ourselves in the Hilton Hotel, life should have been sweet – not so. Kay and Carol were in the Hilton London, Rob and I in the Hilton KL. Good start, with a twenty four hour delay we set off for Singapore, ladies in tow! It wasn't until the customs man came round to check the passports Rob realized his was in his cabin on Britannia. Kay and I were allowed to continue our journey south to Singapore but Rob and Carol had to get off in Jahore at the border. Not being met by our tour operator at the station only compounded what had been a very tiring day. Luckily the Commodore's wife was on the station platform and came to our rescue with the loan of a twenty dollar Singapore note, the least we could do was let her have our taxi as she was behind us in the queue with children. I would meet Britannia in the morning and smooth things out with LtCdr Paul Gorsuch another new boss, giving him Rob's most profound apologies, and rescue Rob's passport in the process. The boss would have to do the biggest money changing ever in the Yacht's history, but luckily not alone. Fletch had now been rated PO and with Simmo I'm sure he couldn't have wanted for any more support. It was no hanging about for Kay and I, it was back to Jahore by train to rescue Rob and Carol, and at 2000 that night we were in our hotel and laughing about it, well Rob was as he said 'for rescuing us I'll buy dinner' and I said 'I'll buy the drinks' which turned out to be twice the price of the food – nice one.

We flew to Bangkok for a couple of nights before heading off to Koh Samui where we would be joined by the Boss. Rob left a bottle of wine on his balcony as a peace offering, but I don't think the Boss was harbouring a grudge.

Once back in Singapore, it was good bye to the girls and back onboard to take the flack that always followed a bit of station leave. It must have been hell for those with kids at school, and no possible way of getting their wives out to join them. Financially the Navy were offering an interest free loan over ten months which I thought was brilliant value, but of course both Kay and I were both in work, and could take advantage of it. For those where only one parent was working or they couldn't get time away from children, it was a no go from the start.

## JAPAN

Of all the places in the world I had wanted to visit since joining the Navy, I was to do it in my last year at sea, calling at Bangkok and Manila for commercial receptions, before arriving in Tokyo. It was a thrill and a disappointment both at the same time, I was expecting the big buildings of Electric City, but what I didn't see was any rice paper houses or Geisha girls. Perhaps that would all come later. We had been assigned a guard ship from the Japanese Navy, and although their crew didn't speak any English and us no Japanese, we got on well enough to split a few of bottles of Sake, too many in fact. They would stay with us all our time in Japanese waters, only leaving us for a brief time whilst we visited Inchon in South Korea. My only memory of Inchon is a meal ashore with Rob. We both had the sea cucumber, I didn't know which end to put on the loo for nearly eight hours, Rob nothing - how unfair.

We hosted commercial receptions in Nagoya and Kobe before calling in at Okinawa for just a port visit so the crew could wind down. It had been a very busy time; I had never done so much washing up in my life!

## HONG KONG

If the atmosphere was electric the weather was awful. With massed bands and much pomp witnessed by Prince Charles, Chris Patten, Steve Green and myself, oh and half the known world, the Union Flag was lowered on yet another British Colony. With rain bouncing off umbrellas, and most of it from the chap behind me running down my neck, we witnessed the handover before having to run very quickly back to Britannia, for the last ceremonial departure. We sailed out fully floodlit, and anyone witnessing this small flotilla of ships, couldn't have failed to be moved. Perhaps the sun had finally set on the British Empire.

We would land Prince Charles and the Patten family off in Manila, but not before the Commander would stitch up seven Yachtsmen well and truly, myself included. A notice had been put around the Yacht looking for dog carers for the Patten's dogs (whisky and soda). I hadn't seen any dogs being brought onboard during our time in Hong Kong so should have been wiser. Being called to the Commanders cabin and briefed when and where we could walk them. With Commander Martin leading we were taken to where the dogs were supposedly kennelled, only to find on our arrival that the whole Yacht's company had been gathered, and was now having a laugh at our expense. Being armed with a 'poop scoop' supplied by the Commander, there was only one thing to do, I grabbed the Commander's wedding tackle in the poop scoop and gave a gentle squeeze. We'd been well and truly had. The following flyer was going round the Messes, obviously the Band were preparing early for the trip home.

INTER- MESS
SUEZ DUVET CHALLENGE
162 KM OF PURE SLEEPING1 ARE YOU TIRED
ENOUGH TO FACE THE CHALLENGE???
You have to be **IN IT** to win it
Don't refuse to Snooze
Chicks Dig Big Eyelids!!
SEE ANY MEMBER OF THE BAND FOR
AN ENTRY FORM AND ADVICE

## THE LAST LONG JOURNEY HOME

The twenty five day passage would pass quickly, with so much having been arranged in the way of entertainment. Everything from horse racing with wooden horses and large dice in buckets, to a full blown village fete complete with stalls and volunteer band was held on the Royal deck, and the thing I had been waiting for 'The Raffle'. Since sailing from UK with the help of Simmo, Fletch, Mark and Andy I had been selling tickets and buying prizes in every port of call. The prize total was in excess of £4,500 pounds, which made this the biggest and best raffle in the Yacht's history. I had run a couple of raffles in the past and it had been hard to get over the 'Bo legacy', but by borrowing money from the Welfare fund and buying prizes up front I had finally managed to convince the crew there would be more than a 'television and painted egg complete with insect farm'. The draw took place at the end of the fete and was a resounding success.

The rest of the evenings of the voyage home would be games nights in the wardroom, Warrant and CPO's mess, Tombola in the Unwinding room, and very many laps of the upper deck wearing brand new running kit. I had let Rob talk me into running the Rock of

Gibraltar on our last visit. The day of the race came and we both ran in together in a very respectable 34 minutes and 11 seconds, and I'm glad to say' for the very last time'. I had first done the Rock race on the way down South on HMS Endurance in both 1976/77, twenty years later and I was still trying to prove something.

## THE SUMMER BALL

Making our way down to Portsmouth with our neighbours, travelling in his four wheel drive, we hadn't gone forty miles when a loud bang from under the bonnet, put pay to our early arrival. Luckily Claude owned a transport firm, and casually just phoned and said 'send out a low loader with the Audi' and gave the location. His wife Jackie turned and said 'Claude – it's at times like these, I'm glad you not a Jeweller'. We flew the rest of the journey at zero feet in the Quattro with our baggage and finery on our knees, arriving only an hour later than planned. Only two things didn't make the journey Claude's cuff links and most importantly his Black shores. The former we could cure with a phone call, the later he would have to put up with, full black tie and brown shoes – nice. We met up with all the other's staying overnight in the 'Ibis' and had a drink whilst waiting for the taxi. What we hadn't told our wives or guests, is that we had hired a stretch limo to do a shuttle run. A perfect evening was had by all, with Claude keeping his feet under the table unless it was just for a dance.

If the night went okay it was the morning that sorted the men from the boys. All PO's were required to turn up in the morning to return Britannia to some semblance of order. All chairs, tables and a dance floor had to be taken apart and moved to the jetty. I could understand now why we didn't have a summer ball on a more regular occasion. The Warrants and Chiefs would put the whole thing together in the cold light of day and in Yacht time, but on a Sunday morning with only eight PO's turning up to take it all apart, and all having a very late night the night before was almost a bridge too far. Claude wouldn't believe when we met in the morning at 1100 that I had been back onboard for two hours helping out. I swear the band had still been playing in my head, but what did happen to the other twenty two PO's?

## THE FAREWELL TRIP AROUND BRITAIN

The very last Western Isles cruise would see more of the Royal family onboard than normal, and everything was starting to seem so final. It was all 'we won't be back here, won't see that again, and move on to the next port'.  Lots of the Yacht's company like me were hoping that Britannia would call into a port near their home, so they could get family and friends onboard. I was hoping for Ramsgate but the closest we would get is London. I invited as many people onboard as was possible, squeezing them in between the Royal Duties life was as hectic as ever.

We sailed into Portsmouth out of a mist, with fire tender's hoses spraying to Port and Starboard, and aircraft flying overhead. Our paying off pennant, close to four hundred feet long, instead of trailing majestically behind us refused to fly in the light winds, and sort of lay sick on the deck. Kay for once was on the jetty to witness Britannia's arrival, and along with everyone one else was moved by the spectacle of Britannia, but more so by the wet eyes of her crew. Having now got onboard to witness people returning from Harbour Stations to the mess, Alf entered tears on his cheek's still reflecting on the Commodore's last order. **'Finished with engines'**

A government that had told the country the cost of everything and the value of nothing had its way; no longer did Britannia rule the waves. For the first time since Charles II Britain has no Royal Yacht.

## PAYING OFF

It had been customary in the past for Her Majesty to grant an audience to Yachtsmen who had served for over ten years onboard, and this practise was to be continued to the last. Lining up in the Royal Dining Room, we were ushered in one by one into the Queen's study, to stand before Her Majesty the Queen and the Duke of Edinburgh. They asked how long you had served onboard, and what job you had done, and where you were going now. With much thanks for Service on Britannia, good luck for the future, presentation of a signed photograph, and a handshake from both, my audience was over.

Some of the crew were only a few months short of ten years service like Squiffy and would not qualify for an audience or photograph, but I believe to this day a signed photograph, not even presented by Her Majesty would have been a fitting final gesture for their efforts.

On the 11$^{th}$ of December in front of the Royal Family, a large crowd of Past Yachtsmen and wives on the Jetty, and the rest of the World watching on television, Her Majesty's Royal Yacht Britannia bowed out, nearly five hundred years of history gone. With the Yacht's Company manning the side for the last time, Royal Marine Band playing on the Jetty as they marched up and down, Captain David Cole (DOM) saluted us all as they marched off to the tune 'A Life on the Ocean Wave'

A reunion buffet style dinner was held on South railway Jetty opposite Britannia that evening, and although those attending had a good time, it was more for sea stories and reflection. Many like Kay and I didn't attend the Yachtsmen's Dance held ashore on the Saturday, preferring to slip away onto Christmas leave.

Before returning from Christmas leave, all eyes would be scanning the papers for the New Years Honours List. The Royal Victoria Medal presented for loyal service to the Crown being the object of their desire. When the Royal Flight had paid off there seemed to be more than normal on the list, with Britannia's demise it didn't seem to be the case. There was the odd happy face onboard, but for every one of those there were ten not smiling. To those that were successful – well done chaps.

## DESTORE 1998

With work starting immediately on running down Britannia, the first thing to go was hotel services. With no heads, showers, galleys or heating, there was only one place to be – HMS Nelson Barracks. A single cabin being luxury to the gulch quarters we had endured onboard.
We would need, and have, six weeks to strip out everything that was remotely Royal or Royal Navy. Anything Royal again was taken off to the Palaces, being securely wrapped by the Royal Stewards before being moved onto removal lorries, and no Household Cavalry this time.
Naval Stores were only responsible for the contents of the storerooms, and what was held independently by over fifty different departments.

With Andy Geoff and I working flat out and being overseen by a Civilian from Naval Base Supply Agency the Yacht started to spill its character ashore at an alarming rate. Wardroom, Warrant and

Chiefs, PO's and Unwinding room had been given instructions from the Palace to auction or Raffle any mess owned property. Ammunition and Weapons, fuel, water and oil tanks all now stood empty. The warrants and Chiefs and PO's messes now just used for Stand Easy forenoon and afternoon. The home of Bunny hops, the four o clock club, Tombola and so many endless evenings of fun the Unwinding Room looking the saddest of them all, with its stripped out display cabinets, copper table tops and not a signed picture of the Royal Family on the bulkheads, it was enough to make you weep.

Although work carried on to prepare Britannia for handover, the atmosphere in the mixed Senior Rates mess in HMS Nelson, was as though nothing had happened. Meeting every night for a beer after supper to discuss how things were progressing. Squiffy, Ginge, Verne, I and sometimes Alf, would talk as if we were just waiting for the reprieve. It was of course never to come, and on the 27th February 1998 after Alf turned off the lights, the Commodore, Alf and I were the last to leave. The Commodore locked the gangway gate and threw what we thought were the keys into the basin saying 'we won't need those again'

## WASHUP AND DE-BRIEF

In the 4,186 days I served onboard, I had travelled over 300,000 miles, shown hundreds of people around from almost every country in the world, and paid the bar bill out of my own pocket, as did every Yachtsman who let his parrot go off 'Come onboard- Come onboard'.

What I miss the most as I reflect back on half a Naval Career is the people I served with and what I was serving for. To feel your own chest heave with pride when the band play, as you watch the White Ensign flutter on the mast. To have my bottom lip quiver and knees knock when being approached by a member of the Royal family. To say to everyone 'I am proud to serve Her Majesty – not only have I met them, I've been 'Up Homers'.

Also what has gone is the camaraderie that can only come with an institution that has been run by its own inmates for over 400 years.

Never to hear Alex Shenton playing the optics behind the bar and when asked to close it saying, 'this isn't a bar – it's a musical instrument'.
Nigel Sullivan when asked what he wants from the Naafi, and his reply being 'Cats a$@hole for me cheers' his name for a sausage roll.
Hearing Squiffy say 'this beer is like singing hymns, an Angel peeing on my tonsils', after a long hot day caulking the upper deck.

Al J relaying his Tombola numbers 62 – 78 e.g. clickerty duckerty – crutcherty bollock (Clickerty being six, duckerty being 2, crutcherty being 7 and bollock an 8) all done at speed - amazing.

Lastly for Ginge who insisted on buying his own polish for the engine room, saying 'All you can give me is rubbish, I'll buy me own'.

So all gone chaps – good whilst it lasted
If I have taken your name in vain – **sorry**, if I put you in the frame for something you did not do – **very sorry**. If I have miss quoted or got the dit or date wrong – **really very sorry**. If I haven't named you I'm even sorrier, you must have done something I missed.

It was never the intention for this to read as a stitch up, in fact it was written in HMS Nelson in 1998/9, and after being re-called for service with the Army in Kosovo 2000 as a journal of my life called 'Under sailing Orders' which I never published.

I still live in Monkton, on my beloved Isle of Thanet, which I wouldn't swop for anywhere in the World; it is my piece of England in God's Country. Simon my very good friend and neighbour, who looked out for Kay whilst I was at sea, is still a very close mate, thanks - I owe you big time, but can I have the shed key back!

Matt (Snaps) and I meet up at least once a year, in our tin tents on wheels (caravans), with the wives in tow, and laugh about old times.

Have the years been kind, I hope they have to all of you. As for me they were right about medals and piles, they just forgot to mention the arthritis and tinnitus, still chin up, it's not all a pain in the a@~e.

## For the uninitiated

| | |
|---|---|
| AB | Able rate – Sailor |
| ADRIFT | Late for Duty |
| AFT | Rear of ship – the blunt bit |
| BOSUN | Seaman Officer |
| BULKHEAD | Interior wall of ship |
| BUFFER | Chief Bosun's mate – Chief Sailor |
| BURMA ROAD | Main passageway in ship or Yacht |
| CDR | Commander |
| CIVVY STREET | Civilian life - Civvies clothing |
| CLUB SWINGER | Physical training Instructor |
| COLOURS | Raising the Ensign/Jack in the morning |
| CORY | Commodore of Royal Yacht's |
| COX'N | Person in charge of discipline and routines |
| CPL | Corporal |
| CPO | Chief Petty Officer |
| DEADLIGHT | Covering plate for a scuttle |
| DITS | Naval tales – sea stories |
| DO | Divisional Officer |
| DOG WATCHES | 1600 – 1800 / 1800 – 200 |
| DOM | Director of music |
| FOC'SLE | Front of ship – the pointy bit |
| FOR'ARD | Forward of Midships – the middle |
| FORY | Flag Officer of Royal Yachts |
| GREENIE | Electrician |
| GRIP | Weekend Bag |
| GRIPPO | A very nice person who buys the drinks |
| GULCH | Bed space |
| GUZZ | Plymouth in Devon |
| HANDS | Sailors |
| HEADS | Toilets |
| JACK DUSTY | Storeman |
| KILLICK | Leading Hand (similar to Corporal in Army) * |
| LEADING RATE | Killick                                   * |

| | |
|---|---|
| LSA | Leading Store Accountant |
| MAN SHIP | Ceremony of lining the Yacht's side |
| MUSN | Musician |
| NAAFI | Naval Army Air Force Institute (Canteen) |
| NINES | Naval Punishment – stoppage of Leave |
| NO 1's | Gold Badge Uniform |
| OPPO | Close friend or shipmate |
| PIPE THE SIDE | Ceremony given to Commanding Officer (in the case of Britannia the Monarch) |
| PMO | Principal Medical Officer |
| PO's | Petty Officers |
| POMPEY | Portsmouth |
| PONGO | Soldier |
| PTI | Physical training Instructor (Clubs) |
| RABBITS | Souvenirs |
| R & R | Rest and Recuperation |
| RIG | Uniform |
| ROUNDS | Inspection by Command of whole ship |
| SCRAN | Breakfast, dinner or supper |
| SCUTTLE | Porthole |
| SEA DAYS | Commercial business days |
| SGT | Sergeant |
| SNAPS | Naval Photographer |
| SODS OPERA | A complete farce |
| STEAMING BOOTS | Steel toe capped black work boots |
| STOKER | Marine engineering mechanic |
| SUNSET | Lowering of the Ensign/Jack at night |
| S & S | Supply and Secretarial branch of the Navy |
| TRAP | Sit down cubicle in toilet |
| TSF | Total Steam failure – Stokers nightmare |
| TYS | Through Your Scuttle – Video show |
| UCKERS | A sailors game of ludo |
| UP HOMERS | The ultimate Grippo – home for a meal |
| WOWTR | Warrant Officer Writer |
| YEOMAN | Flag Wagger – Bunting Tosser |